CONTENTS

Introduction 5
1 The Lack Of Prayer 13
2 The Working Of The Spirit And Prayer 21
3 A Model Of Intercession 30
4 Because Of His Importunity 39
5 The Life That Can Pray 48
2 Restraining Prayer—Is It Sin? 58
7 Who Shall Deliver? 67
8 Wilt Thou Be Made Whole 77
9 The Secret Of Effectual Prayer 87
10 The Spirit Of Supplication 96
11 In The Name Of Christ 106
12 My God Will Hear Me 117
13 Paul, A Pattern Of Prayer 126
14 God Seeks Intercessors 137
15 The Coming Revival 146
   Helps To Intercession 155
   The Ministry Of Intercession 201

INTRODUCTION

A friend, who heard that this book was being published, asked how it differed from my previous one on the same subject, *With Christ in the School of Prayer*. An answer to that question may be the best introduction I can give to the present volume.

Any acceptance the former work has had must be attributed, as far as the contents go, to the prominence it gives to two great truths: The first is the certainty that prayer will be answered. Some believe that to ask and expect an answer is not the highest form of prayer. They maintain that fellowship with God is more than supplication, which is often selfish. To worship is more than to beg. With others, the thought that prayer is so often unanswered is so prominent, that they think more of the spiritual benefit derived from the exercise of prayer than the actual gifts to be obtained by it. While admitting the measure of truth in these views, when kept in their true place, *The School of Prayer* points out how our Lord continually spoke of prayer as a means of obtaining what we desire. It illustrates how He seeks in every possible way to awaken in us the confident expectation of an answer to prayer. I was led to show how prayer—in which a man could enter into the mind of God, could assert the royal power of a renewed will, and bring down to earth what, without prayer, would not have been given—is the highest proof of man having been made in the likeness of God's Son. He is found worthy of entering into fellowship with Him, not only in adoration and worship, but in having his will actually taken up into the rule of the world, and becoming the intelligent channel through which God can fulfill His eternal purpose. The book sought to reiterate and enforce the precious truths Christ preaches so continually: the blessing of prayer is that you can ask and receive what you will; the highest exercise and the glory of prayer is that persevering importunity can prevail and obtain what God at first could not and would not give.

With this truth there was a second one that came out very strongly as we studied the Master's words. In answer to the question, But why, if the answer to prayer is so positively promised, are there such numerous unanswered prayers? we found that Christ taught us that the answer depended upon certain conditions. He spoke of faith, of perseverance, of praying in His Name, of praying in the will of God. But all these conditions were summed up in the central one: "*if ye abide in Me*, ask whatsoever ye will and it shall be done unto you." It became clear that the power to pray the effectual prayer of faith depended *upon the life*. It is only to a man given up to live as entirely *in* Christ and *for* Christ as the branch in the vine and for the vine, that these promises can come true. *"In that day,"* Christ said, the day

6

of Pentecost, "ye shall ask in My Name." It is only in a life full of the Holy Spirit that the true power to ask in Christ's Name can be known. This led to the emphasizing of the truth that the ordinary Christian life cannot appropriate these promises. It needs a spiritual life, altogether sound and vigorous, to pray in power. The teaching naturally led to press the need of a life of entire consecration. More than one person has told me how it was in the reading of the book that he first saw what the better life was that could be lived, and must be lived, if Christ's wonderful promises are to come true to us.

In regard to these two truths, there is no change in the present volume. One only wishes that one could present them with such clearness and force as to help every beloved fellow-Christian to some right impression of the reality and the glory of our privilege as God's children: "Ask whatsoever ye will, and it shall be done unto you." The present volume owes its existence to the desire to enforce two truths, of which formerly I had no such impression as now.

The one is—that Christ actually meant prayer to be the great power by which His Church should do its work, and that the neglect of prayer is the great reason the Church has not greater power over the masses in Christian and in heathen countries. In the first chapter, I have stated how my convictions in regard to this have been strengthened, and what gave occasion to the writing of the book. It is meant to be, on behalf of myself and my brethren in the ministry and all God's people, a confession of shortcoming and of sin. At the same time, it is a call to believe that things can be different, and that Christ waits to fit us by His Spirit to pray as He would have us. This call, of course, brings me back to what I spoke of in connection with the former volume: that there is a life in the Spirit, a life of abiding in Christ, within our reach, in which the power of prayer—both the power to pray and the power to obtain the answer—can be realized in a measure which we could not have thought possible before. Any failure in the prayer life, any desire or hope really to take the place Christ has prepared for us, brings us to the very root of the doctrine of grace as manifested in the Christian life. It is only by a full surrender to the life of abiding, by the yielding to the fullness of the Spirit's leading and quickening, that the prayer life can be restored to a truly healthy state. I feel deeply how little I have been able to put this in the volume as I could wish. I have prayed and am trusting that God, who chooses the weak things, will use it for His own glory.

The second truth which I have sought to enforce is that we have far too little conception of the place that intercession, as distinguished from prayer for ourselves, ought to have in the Church and the Christian life. In intercession, our King upon the throne finds His highest glory; in it we will find our highest glory, too. Through it, He continues His saving work, and can do nothing without it; through it alone we can do our work, and nothing avails without it. In it, He ever receives from the Father the

8

Holy Spirit and all spiritual blessings to impart; in it we too are called to receive in ourselves the fullness of God's Spirit, with the power to impart spiritual blessing to others. The power of the Church to truly bless rests on intercession—asking and receiving heavenly gifts to carry to men. Because this is so, it is no wonder that where—owing to lack of teaching or spiritual insight—we put the trust in our own diligence and effort—to the influence of the world and the flesh—and work more than we pray, the presence and power of God are not seen in our work as we would wish.

Such thoughts have led me to wonder what could be done to rouse believers to a sense of their high calling in this, and to help and train them to take part in it. And so this book differs from the former one in the attempt to open a practicing school, and to invite all who have never taken systematic part in the great work of intercession to begin and give themselves to it. There are tens of thousands of workers who have known and are proving wonderfully what prayer can do. But there are tens of thousands who work with little prayer. There are many more who do not work at all because they do not know how or where they might all be added to the host of intercessors who are to bring down the blessings of heaven to earth. For their sakes, and the sake of all who feel the need of help, I have prepared helps and hints for a school of intercession for a month at the end of this book.

I have asked those who want to join to begin by

giving at least ten minutes a day to this work. It is in doing that we learn to do; it is as we take hold and begin that the help of God's Spirit will come. It is as we daily hear God's call, and at once put it into practice, that the consciousness will begin to live in us—I too am an intercessor. We will feel the need of living in Christ and being full of the Spirit if we do this work correctly. Nothing will so test and stimulate the Christian life as the honest attempt to be an intercessor. It is difficult to conceive of how much we ourselves and the Church will gain if, with our whole heart, we accept the post of honor God is offering us. With regard to the school of intercession, I am confident that the result of the first month's course will be to awaken the feeling of how little we know how to intercede. And a second and a third month may only deepen the sense of ignorance and unfitness. This will be an unspeakable blessing. The confession, "We know not how to pray as we ought," is the introduction to the experience, "The Spirit maketh intercession for us." Our sense of ignorance will lead us to depend on the Spirit praying in us, to feel the need of living in the Spirit.

We have heard a great deal about systematic Bible study, and we praise God for thousands and thousands of Bible classes and Bible readings. Let all the leaders of such classes try to start prayer classes—helping their students to pray in secret, and training them to be, above everything, men of prayer. Let ministers ask what they can do in this. The faith in God's Word can nowhere be so exercised and perfected as in the intercession that asks, expects, and looks out for the answer. Throughout Scripture, in the life of every saint, of God's own Son, throughout the history of God's Church, God is, first of all, a prayer-hearing God. Let us try and help God's children to know their God, and encourage all God's servants to labor with the assurance: the chief and most blessed part of my work is to ask and receive from my Father what I can bring to others.

It will now easily be understood that what this book contains will be nothing but the confirmation and the call to put into practice the two great lessons of the former one. *"Ask whatsoever ye will, and it shall be done to you"; "Whatever ye ask, believe that ye have received."* These great prayer-promises, as part of the Church's enduement of power for her work, are to be taken as literally and actually true. *"If ye abide in Me, and My words abide in you"; "In that day ye shall ask in My Name."* These great prayer-conditions are universal and unchangeable. A life abiding in Christ and filled with the Spirit, a life entirely given up as a branch for the work of the vine, has the power to claim these promises, and to pray the effectual prayer that avails much. Lord, teach us to pray.

Andrew Murray

Chapter 1

THE LACK OF PRAYER

"Ye have not, because ye ask not"—James 4:2.

"And He saw that there was no man, and wondered that there was no intercessor"—Isaiah 59:16.

"There is none that calleth upon Thy name, that stirreth up himself to take hold of Thee"—Isaiah 64:7.

The entire morning session of a convention I recently attended was devoted to prayer and intercession. Great blessing was found, both in listening to what the Word teaches of their need and power, and in joining in continued, united supplication. Many felt that we knew too little of persevering, importunate prayer, and that it is, indeed, one of the greatest needs of the Church.

We pray too little! There is even a lack of hope for any great change, due to force of habit, and the pressured feeling that prayer is a duty.

What I have heard lately regarding prayer has made a deep impression on me. What affected me

13

the most was that God's servants should feel hopeless about the prospect of an entire change being made. I prayed God would give me words that might help to direct attention to the problem and to stir up faith, awakening the assurance that God, by His Spirit, will enable us to pray as we should. Real deliverance can be found from a failure which hinders our own joy in God, and our power in His service.

Let me begin, for the sake of those who have never had their attention directed to the matter, by giving some examples that prove how universal the sense of shortcoming in prayer is.

Dr. Whyte, of Free St. George's, Edinburgh, made an address to ministers. In it, he said that, as a young minister, he had thought that he should spend as much of his free time as possible with his books in his study. This was because he wanted to feed his people with the very best he could prepare for them. But he had now learned that prayer was of more importance than study. He remembered that deacons were elected to take charge of the collections, so that the apostles could "give themselves to prayer and the ministry of the word." At times, when the deacons of his congregation brought him his salary, he had to ask himself whether he had been as faithful in his responsibilities as they had been in theirs. He felt as if it were almost too late to regain what he had lost, and urged his brethren to pray more. What a solemn confession and warning from one of the high places: We pray too little!

14

During a convention several years ago, I was discussing the subject of prayer in conversation with a well-known London minister. He maintained that if so much time must be given to prayer, it would involve the neglect of the responsibilities of his position. "There is the morning mail, before breakfast, with ten or twelve letters which *must* be answered. Then there are committee meetings waiting, with countless other engagements, more than enough to fill up the day. It is difficult to see how it can all be done."

My answer was, in substance, that it was simply a question of whether the call of God for our time and attention was of more importance than that of man. If God was waiting to meet us, and to give us blessing and power from heaven for His work, it was a shortsighted policy to put other work in the place which God and waiting on Him should have.

At one of our ministerial meetings, the superintendent of a large district put the case this way: "I rise in the morning and, before breakfast, have half an hour with God, in the Word and in prayer. I go out and am occupied all day with a multiplicity of engagements. I do not think many minutes elapse without my breathing a prayer for guidance or help. After my day's work, I return in my evening devotions and speak to God about the day's work. But of the intense, definite, importunate prayer of which Scripture speaks, I know little." What, he asked, must I think of such a life?

Imagine the difference between a man whose

profits are just enough to maintain his family and keep up his business, and another whose income enables him to extend the business and to help others. There can be an earnest Christian life in which there is prayer enough to keep us from backsliding, just maintaining the position we have, without much growth in spirituality or Christlikeness. This prayer attitude is more defensive—seeking to ward off temptation—than aggressive, reaching out after higher attainment. If we are to grow in strength, with some large experience of God's power to sanctify ourselves and to bring down real blessing on others, there must be more definite and persevering prayer. The Scripture, teaching about "crying day and night"; "continuing steadfastly in prayer"; "watching unto prayer"; "being heard for his importunity," must, in some degree, become our experience if we are really to be intercessors.

Another example: A pastor of quite a large church who had many responsibilities once said to me, "I see the importance of much prayer, and yet my life hardly leaves room for it. Are we to submit? Or tell us how we can attain what we desire?" I admitted that the difficulty was universal. A most honored South African missionary, now gone to his rest, had the same complaint. I recalled his words: "In the morning at five, the sick people are at the door waiting for medicine. At six, the printers come, and I have to set them to work and teach them. At nine, the school calls me, and, till late at night, I am kept busy with a large correspondence."

In my answer, I quoted a Dutch proverb: " 'What *is* heaviest must *weigh* heaviest'—must have the first place." The law of God is unchangeable; as on earth, so in our traffic with heaven, we only get as we give. Unless we are willing to pay the price, and sacrifice time, attention, and what appear legitimate or necessary duties for the sake of the heavenly gifts, we need not look for a large experience of the power of the heavenly world in our work. The whole company present joined in the sad confession; it had been thought over, and mourned over, times without number. Yet, somehow, there they were, all these pressing claims, and all the ineffectual resolves to pray more, barring the way. I do not need to say to what further thoughts our conversation led; the substance of them will be found in some of the later chapters in this volume.

Let me call just one more witness. In the course of my journey, I met with one of the Cowley Fathers who had just been holding Retreats for clergy of the English Church. I was interested to hear from him the line of teaching he follows. In the course of conversation, he used the expression—"the distraction of business," and it came out that he found it one of the great difficulties he had to deal with in himself and others. Of himself, he said that by the vows of his Order he was bound to give himself specially to prayer. But he found it exceedingly difficult. Every day he had to be at four different points of the town he lived in; his predecessor had left him the charge of a number of committees where he was expected to do all the work. It was as if everything conspired to keep him from prayer.

All this testimony clarifies the fact that prayer does not have the place it should have in our ministerial and Christian life. The shortcoming is one of which all are willing to confess, and the difficulties in the way of deliverance are such as to make a return to a true and full prayer life almost impossible. Blessed be God—"The things that are impossible with men are possible with God!" "God is able to make all grace abound toward you, that ye, always having all sufficiency in all things, may abound to all good work." Do let us believe that God's call to much prayer need not be a burden and cause of continual self-condemnation. He means it to be a joy. He can make it an inspiration, giving us strength for all our work, and bringing down His power to work through us in our fellow-men. Do not be afraid to fully admit to the sin that shames us, and then to face it in the name of our Mighty Redeemer. *The light that shows us our sin and condemns us for it, will show us the way out of it into the life of liberty that is well-pleasing to God*. If we allow this one matter, unfaithfulness in prayer, to convict us of the lack in our Christian life, God will use the discovery to bring us not only the power to pray that we long for, but the joy of a new and healthy life, of which prayer is the spontaneous expression.

And what is the way by which our sense of the lack of prayer can be made the means of blessing, the entrance on a path in which the evil may be conquered? How can our fellowship with the Father, in continual prayer and intercession, become what it ought to be, if we and the world around us are to be blessed? As it appears to me, we must begin by going back to God's Word, to study what *place God means prayer to have* in the life of His child and His Church. A fresh sight of what prayer is *according to the will of God*, of what our prayers can be, *through the grace of God*, will free us from those feeble, defective views in regard to the absolute necessity of continual prayer, which lie at the root of our failure. As we get an insight into the reasonableness and rightness of this Divine appointment, and come under the full conviction of how wonderfully it fits in with God's love and our own happiness, we will be freed from the false impression of its being an arbitrary demand. With our whole heart and soul, we will consent to it and rejoice in it, as the only possible way for the blessing of heaven to come to earth. All thought of task and burden, of self-effort and strain, will pass away in the blessed faith that as simple as breathing is in the healthy, natural life, will praying be in the Christian life that is led and filled by the Spirit of God.

As we occupy ourselves with and accept this teaching of God's Word on prayer, we will be led to see how our failure in the prayer life was owing to failure in the Spirit-life. Prayer is one of the most heavenly and spiritual of the functions of the Spirit-life. How could we try or expect to fulfill it so as to please God, except as our soul is in perfect health, and our life truly possessed and moved by God's Spirit? The insight into the place God means prayer to have, and which it only *can* have in a full Christian life, will show us that we have not been living the true, the abundant life. It will show us that any thought of praying more and effectually will be vain, except as we are brought into a closer relationship with our Blessed Lord Jesus.

Christ is our life. Christ lives in us in such reality that His life of prayer on earth, and of intercession in heaven, is breathed into us in just such measure as our surrender and our faith allow and accept it. Jesus Christ is the Healer of all diseases, the Conqueror of all enemies, the Deliverer from all sin. If our failure teaches us to turn afresh to Him, and to find in Him the grace He gives to pray as we should, this humiliation may become our greatest blessing. Let us all unite in praying to God, that He would visit our souls and fit us for that work of intercession, which is at this moment the greatest need of the Church and the world. It is only by intercession that that power can be brought down from heaven, which will enable the Church to conquer the world. Let us stir up the slumbering gift that is lying unused, and seek to gather, train, and band together as many as we can to be God's remembrancers, and to give Him no rest until He makes His Church a joy in the earth. Nothing but intense, believing prayer can meet the intense spirit of worldliness, which is complained of everywhere.

Chapter 2

THE WORKING OF THE SPIRIT AND PRAYER

"If ye then, being evil, know how to give good gifts unto your children: how much more shall your heavenly Father give the Holy Spirit to them that ask Him?"—Luke 11:13.

Christ had just said in Luke 11:9, "Ask, and it shall be given." God's giving is inseparably connected with our asking. He applies this especially to the Holy Spirit. As surely as a father on earth gives bread to his child, so God gives the Holy Spirit to them that ask Him. The whole working of the Spirit is ruled by one great law: God must give it and we must ask for it. When the Holy Spirit was poured out at Pentecost with a flow that never ceases, it was in answer to prayer. The inflow into the believer's heart, and His outflow in the rivers of living water, still depend on the law: "Ask, and it shall be given."

In connection with our confession of the lack of prayer, what we need is some understanding of the place it occupies in God's plan of redemption.

21

Nowhere is this seen more clearly than in the first half of the Acts of the Apostles. The story of the birth of the Church in the outpouring of the Holy Spirit, and of the first freshness of its heavenly life in the power of that Spirit, will teach us how *prayer on earth*, whether as cause or effect, *is the true measure of the presence of the Spirit of heaven.*

We begin with the well-known words (Acts 1:14) "These all continued with one accord in prayer and supplication." And, further, from chapter 2: "And when the day of Pentecost was fully come, they were all with one accord in one place.... And they were all filled with the Holy Ghost.... And the same day there were added unto them about three thousand souls." The great work of redemption had been accomplished. The Holy Spirit had been promised by Christ "not many days hence." He had sat down on His throne and received the Spirit from the Father. But all this was not enough. One thing more was needed: the disciples' ten days of united, continued supplication. It was intense, continued prayer that prepared the disciples' hearts, opened the windows of heaven, and brought down the promised gift. The power of the Spirit could no more be given without Christ sitting on the throne than it *could descend without the disciples on the footstool of the throne.* For all ages, the law is laid down here, at the birth of the Church, that the power of the Spirit must be prayed down from heaven. The amount of believing, continued prayer will determine the amount of the Spirit's working in the Church.

22

Direct, definite, determined prayer is what we need.

See how this is confirmed in Acts, chapter 4. Peter and John had been brought before the Council and threatened with punishment. When they returned to their brethren, and reported what had been said to them, "they lifted up their voice to God with one accord," and prayed for boldness to speak the Word. "And when they had prayed, the place was shaken...and they were all filled with the Holy Ghost, and they spake the word of God with boldness. And the multitude of them that believed were of one heart and one soul...And with great power gave the apostles witness of the resurrection of the Lord Jesus: and great grace was upon them all." It is as if the story of Pentecost is repeated a second time over—with the prayer, the shaking of the house, the filling with the Spirit, the speaking God's Word with boldness and power, the great grace upon all, and the manifestation of unity and love—to imprint ineffaceably on the heart of the Church that it is prayer which lies at the root of her spiritual life and power. The measure of God's giving the Spirit is our asking. He gives as a father to him who asks as a child.

Go on to Acts, the sixth chapter. There we find that, when murmuring arose as to the neglect of the Grecian Jews in the distribution of alms, the apostles proposed the appointment of deacons to serve the tables. "We," they said, "will give ourselves continually to prayer, and to the ministry of the word." It is often said that there is nothing in honest business, when it is kept in its place as entirely subordinate to the Kingdom, which must ever be first, preventing fellowship with God. Work like ministering to the poor should certainly not hinder the spiritual life. And yet the apostles felt it would hinder them in their giving themselves to the ministry of prayer and the Word. What does this teach? That the maintenance of the spirit of prayer is not enough for those who are the leaders of the Church. To keep the communication between the King and His servants clear and fresh, to draw down power and blessing— not only for the maintenance of our own spiritual life, but for those around us—and to continually receive instruction and empowerment for the great work to be done, the apostles, as the ministers of the Word, felt the need to be free from other duties in order to give themselves to much prayer.

James writes: "Pure religion and undefiled before God and the Father is this, To visit the fatherless and widows in their affliction" (James 1:27). If ever any work were a sacred one, it was that of caring for these Grecian widows. And yet, even these duties might interfere with the apostles' special calling to give themselves to prayer and the ministry of the Word. In the Kingdom of heaven, as on earth, there is power in the division of labor. While some, like the deacons, had to care especially for serving the tables and ministering the alms of the Church here on earth, others had to be set free for that steadfast continuance in prayer which would uninterruptedly secure the downflow of the powers of the heavenly world. The minister of Christ is set apart to give himself as much to prayer as to the ministry of the Word. Faithful obedience to this law is the secret of the Church's power and success. As before, so *after Pentecost*, the apostles were men given up to prayer.

Acts, chapter 8, shows the intimate connection between the Pentecostal gift and prayer, from another point of view. In Samaria, Philip had preached with great blessing, and many had believed. But the Holy Spirit had, as yet, fallen on none of them. The apostles sent down Peter and John to pray for them, that they might receive the Holy Spirit. The power for such prayer was a higher gift than preaching. It was the work of the men who had been in closest contact with the Lord in glory, the work that was essential to the perfection of the life that preaching and baptism, faith and conversion had only begun. Surely of all the gifts of the early Church for which we should long, there is none more needed than the gift of prayer—prayer that brings down the Holy Spirit on believers. This power is given to the men who say, "We will give ourselves to prayer."

The outpouring of the Holy Spirit in the house of Cornelius at Caesarea (Acts 10) provides another testimony to the wondrous interdependence of the action of prayer and the Spirit, and another proof of what will come to a man who has given himself to prayer. Peter went up at midday to pray on the housetop. And what happened? He saw heaven opened, and there came the vision that revealed to him the cleansing of the Gentiles. Then came the message of the three men from Cornelius, a man who "prayed to God alway," and had heard from an angel, "Thy prayers. . .are come up. . .before God." The Spirit said to Peter, "Go with them." It is Peter, praying, to whom the will of God is revealed, to whom guidance is given as to going to Caesarea, and who is brought into contact with a praying and prepared company of hearers. No wonder that in answer to all this prayer a blessing comes beyond all expectation, and the Holy Spirit is poured out upon the Gentiles. A much-praying minister will receive an entrance into God's will he would otherwise know nothing of. He will be brought to praying people where he does not expect them, and will receive blessing above all he asks or thinks. The teaching and the power of the Holy Spirit are both unalterably linked to prayer.

Our next reference will show us faith in the power that the Church's prayer has with its glorified King, as it is found not only in the apostles, but in the Christian community. In Acts 12, we have the story of Peter in prison on the eve of execution. The death of James had aroused the Church to a sense of real danger, and the thought of losing Peter, too, had awakened all her energies. She took herself to prayer: "Prayer was made without ceasing of the Church unto God for him." That prayer achieved much; Peter was delivered. When he came to the house of Mary, he found "many gathered together praying." Stone walls and double chains, soldiers and keepers, and the iron gate all gave way before

26

the power from heaven brought down to his rescue through prayer. The whole power of the Roman Empire, as represented by Herod, was impotent in the presence of the power the Church of the Holy Spirit wielded in prayer. They stood in close and living communication with their Lord in heaven; they knew that the words, "all power is given unto Me," and "Lo I am with you alway" (Matthew 28:18,20), were absolutely true. They had faith in His promise to hear them no matter what they asked. Because of this, they prayed in the assurance that the powers of heaven could work on earth, and would work at their request and on their behalf. The early Church believed in prayer, and practiced it.

Just one more illustration of the place and the blessing of prayer among men filled with the Holy Spirit. In chapter 13, we have the names of five men at Antioch who had given themselves specially to ministering to the Lord with prayer and fasting. Their giving themselves to prayer was not in vain. As they ministered to the Lord, the Holy Spirit met them, and gave them new insight into God's plans. He called them to be fellow-workers with Himself in an undertaking for which He had called Barnabas and Saul. Their part and privilege would be to support these men with renewed fasting and prayer, and to let them go, "sent forth by the Holy Ghost." God in heaven would not send forth His chosen servants without the co-operation of His Church; men on earth were to have a real partnership in the work of God. It was prayer that fitted and prepared them for

27

this. It was to praying men that the Holy Spirit gave authority to do His work and use His name. It was to prayer that the Holy Spirit was given. It is still prayer that is the only secret of true Church expansion, being guided from heaven to find and send forth God-called and God-empowered men. Through prayer, the Holy Spirit will reveal the men He has selected; through prayer, He will give these men the honor of knowing that they are men, "sent forth by the Holy Ghost." It is prayer which is the link between the King on the throne and the Church at His footstool—the human link that has its Divine strength in the power of the Holy Spirit, who comes in answer to it.

As one looks back on these chapters in the history of the early Church, how clear these two great truths stand out: 1) where there is much prayer, there will be much of the Spirit; and 2) where there is much of the Spirit, there will be ever-increasing prayer. So clear is the living connection between the two, that when the Spirit is given in answer to prayer, it awakens more prayer to prepare for the fuller revelation and communication of His Divine power and grace. If prayer was, thus, the power by which the early Church flourished and triumphed, is there any reason why it should not be the one great need of the Church today?

Let these be considered facts in our Church work: 1) Heaven is still as full of stores of spiritual blessing as it was in the apostles' time. 2) God still delights to give the Holy Spirit to "them that ask

Him." 3) Our life and work are still as dependent on the direct impartation of Divine power as they were in those early times. 4) Prayer is still the appointed means for drawing down these heavenly blessings in power on ourselves and those around us. 5) God is still seeking men and women who will, in addition to all their other work of ministering, specially give themselves to persevering prayer.

And we—you, my reader, and I—may have the privilege of offering ourselves to God to labor in prayer, bringing down these blessings to this earth. Let us beseech God to make all this truth so living in us that we will not be able to rest until it has mastered us, and our whole heart becomes so filled with it, that we will regard the practice of intercession as our highest privilege. Let us find in it the only sure measurement for blessing on ourselves, on the Church, and on the world.

Chapter 3

A MODEL OF INTERCESSION

"And he said unto them, Which of you shall have a friend, and shall go unto him at midnight, and say unto him, Friend, lend me three loaves; for a friend of mine in his journey is come unto me, and I have nothing to set before him? And he from within shall answer and say, Trouble me not:...I cannot rise and give thee. I say unto you, Though he will not rise and give him, because he is his friend, yet because of his importunity he will rise and give him as many as he needeth"—Luke 11:5-8.

"I have set watchmen upon thy walls, O Jerusalem, which shall never hold their peace day nor night: ye that make mention of the Lord, keep not silence, and give Him no rest"—Isaiah 62:6-7.

We have seen what power prayer has in the previous chapter. It is the one power on earth that commands the power of heaven. The story of the early days of the Church is God's great object (lesson)—to teach His Church what prayer can do,

30

how it alone, but most surely, can draw down the treasures and powers of heaven into the life on earth.

Let us briefly recall the lessons we learned. Did we not see: 1) that prayer is both indispensable and irresistible? 2) that untold power and blessing are stored for us in heaven? 3) that this power will make us a blessing to men, and fit us to do any work or face any danger? 4) that this power is to be sought in prayer continually and persistently? 5) that those who have the heavenly power can pray it down upon others? 6) that in all the ministries of Christ's Church, prayer is the one secret of success? 7) that it can defy all the power of the world, and fit men to conquer that world for Christ? Yes, it is the power of the heavenly life—the power of God's own Spirit, the power of Omnipotence—that waits for prayer to bring it down.

In all the prayer of the apostles, there was little thought of personal needs or happiness. It was their desire to witness for Christ and bring Him and His salvation to others; it was the thought of God's Kingdom and glory that possessed these disciples. If we desire to be delivered from the sin of neglecting prayer, we must enlarge our hearts for the work of intercession. Praying constantly for ourselves will come to failure. Only in intercession for others will our faith, love, and perseverance be aroused, and the power of the Spirit, which can fit us for saving men, be found.

We are asking how we may become more faithful and successful in prayer; let us see how the Master teaches us, in the parable of the Friend at Midnight. His lesson is that intercession for the needy requires the highest exercise of our power of believing and prevailing prayer. Intercession is the most perfect form of prayer, in that it is the prayer Christ prays on His throne. Let us learn what the elements of true intercession are.

1. *An urgent need.* Here intercession has its origin. The friend came at midnight—an untimely hour. He was hungry, and could not buy bread. If we are to learn to pray properly, we must open our eyes and heart to the need around us.

We often hear of the millions of unsaved souls living in midnight darkness, perishing for lack of the Bread of life. We also hear of the many nominal Christians who are almost as unenlightened and indifferent as those who are unsaved. We see millions in the Christian Church who know little of a walk in the light of God or in the power of a life fed by bread from heaven. We all have our own circles—congregations, schools, friends, missions—in which the great complaint is that the light and life of God are too little known. Surely, if we believe what we profess—that God alone is able to help, that God certainly *will* help in answer to prayer—all this need ought to make us intercessors, people who give their lives to prayer for those around them.

Let us take time to seriously consider this need. Each Christless soul will go down into utter darkness, perishing from hunger, even though there is bread to spare. Unknown millions of souls are dying without the knowledge of Christ. Our own neighbors and friends—souls intrusted to us—are dying without hope. Christians all around us are living a sickly, feeble, and fruitless spiritual life. Surely there is a need for prayer. *Nothing* but prayer to God for help will avail.

2. *The willing love.* The friend took his weary, hungry friend into his house and into his heart, too. He did not excuse himself by saying he had no bread; even though it was midnight, he sent to find some for him. He sacrificed his night's rest and his comfort to find the needed bread. "Love seeketh not its own" (1 Corinthians 13:4). It is the very nature of love to give up and forget self for the sake of others. It takes their needs and makes them its own, finding its real joy in living and dying for others, as Christ did.

It is the love of a mother for her prodigal son that makes her pray for him. The true love in us will become the spirit of intercession. It is possible to do a great deal of faithful, earnest work for our brothers and sisters without having true love for them. Take into consideration a physician who may be thoroughly interested in his patients, yet does not feel any special love for them. This comes from a love of his profession and a high sense of faithfulness to his duty. In the same way, servants of Christ may devote themselves to their work with self-sacrificing enthusiasm, without their Christlike love for souls being strong enough. It is this lack of love that causes so much shortcoming in prayer. Only as our love of diligence and thoroughness in our prayer-work dis-

33

solves in the tender compassion of Christ, will true love begin compelling us to pray. We will then not be able to rest from our work if there are still souls who are not saved. *True love must pray.*

3. *The sense of impotence.* We often speak of the power of love. In one sense, love does not have power; but this truth has its limitations, which must not be forgotten. The strongest love may be utterly impotent. A mother might be willing to give her life for her dying child, and yet not be able to save it. The friend at midnight was most willing to give his friend bread, but he had none. It was this sense of impotence, of his inability to help, that sent him pleading: "My friend is come to me, and *I have nothing* set before him." This sense of impotence with God's servants is the very strength of the life of intercession.

As the consciousness of this thought—"I have nothing to set before them"—takes possession of the minister, missionary, teacher, or worker, intercession will become their only hope and refuge. I may have knowledge and truth, a loving heart, and the readiness to give myself for those under my charge; but I cannot give them the bread of heaven. Despite all my love and zeal, "I have nothing to set before them." Blessed is the man who has made that "I have nothing" the motto of his ministry. As he thinks of the judgment day and the danger in it for unsaved souls, as he realizes that a supernatural power and life is necessary to save men from sin, as he feels his utter inadequacy to give them life, that *"I have nothing"* urges him to pray. When the desolation of hungry souls in the midnight darkness comes upon him, intercession appears to him as his only hope, the one thing in which his love can take refuge.

Let us take this lesson to heart, as a warning to all those who are strong and wise, and for the encouragement of those who are weak: The sense of our impotence is the soul of intercession. The simplest, weakest Christian can pray down blessing from an Almighty God.

4. *The faith in prayer.* What he does not have himself, another can supply. He has a rich friend near, who will be both able and willing to give him bread. He is sure that if he only asks, he will receive. This faith makes him leave his home at midnight. He knows that, when he does not have any to give, he can ask his friend.

We need this simple, confident faith that God will give us what we ask for. Where it really exists, there will be no mistake about whether or not we should pray. God's Word provides everything needed to stir and strengthen such faith in us. Just as the heaven our natural eyes can see is one great ocean of sunshine, with its light and heat, giving beauty and fruitfulness to earth, Scripture shows us God's true heaven, filled with spiritual blessings— Divine light, love, and life, heavenly joy, peace, and power—all shining down on us. It shows us how God is waiting, delighting to bestow these blessings *in answer to prayer.* In a thousand promises and testimonies, it urges us to believe that prayer will be

35

heard, and that what we cannot possibly do ourselves for those whom we want to help, *can be done by prayer*. Have no doubt that prayer will be heard, that, through prayer, the poorest and weakest can dispense blessings to the needy, and that each of us, though poor, may yet be making many rich.

5. *The importunity that prevails*. The faith of the friend meets a sudden and unexpected obstacle: the rich friend refuses to hear—"I cannot rise and give thee." The loving heart had not counted on this disappointment; it cannot accept it. The supplicant presses his threefold plea: here is my needy friend; you have abundance; I am your friend, and refuses to accept a denial. The love that opened his house at midnight, and then left it to seek help, must win.

This is the central lesson of the parable. In our intercession, we may find that there is difficulty and delay with the answer. It may be as if God says, "I cannot...give thee." It is not easy, against all appearances, to maintain our confidence that He will hear, and to persevere in full assurance that we will have what we ask for. And yet, this is what God looks for from us. He so highly prizes our confidence in Him, it is so essentially the highest honor the creature can show the Creator, that He will do anything to train us in the exercise of this trust in Him. Blessed is the man who is not staggered by God's delay or silence or apparant refusal, but is strong in faith, giving glory to God. Such faith perseveres, importunately, if need be, and cannot fail to inherit the blessing.

6. *The certainty of a rich reward.* "I say unto you, . . . because of his importunity he will . . . give him as many as he needeth." If we could only learn to believe in the certainty of an abundant answer! A prophet of old said: "Let not your hands be weak: for *your work shall be rewarded*" (2 Chronicles 15:7). Those who find it difficult to pray should fix their eyes on the reward, and, in faith, learn to trust the Divine assurance that their prayer cannot be in vain. If we can come to believe in God and His faithfulness, intercession will become the very first thing we take refuge in when we seek blessing for others, and the very last thing for which we cannot find time. And it will become a thing of joy and hope, because, all the time we pray, we know that we are sowing seed that will bring forth fruit a hundred-fold. Disappointment is impossible: "I say unto you, . . . he will rise and give him as many as he needeth."

Take courage! Time spent in prayer will yield more than that given to work. Prayer alone gives work its worth and its success. Prayer opens the way for God Himself to do His work in us and through us. Let our chief work, as God's messengers, be intercession; in it, we secure the presence and power of God to go with us.

"Which of you shall have a friend . . . at midnight, and say unto him, Friend, lend me three loaves?" This Friend is none other but our God. Do let us learn that in the darkness of midnight—at the most unlikely time and in our greatest need—when we have "nothing to set before" those we love, we have a rich Friend in heaven, the Everlasting God and Father, who is waiting to be asked for help. Let us confess our lack of prayer before Him, admitting that it proves our weak faith, and is the symptom of a life that is still too much under the power of self, the flesh, and the world. The Lord Jesus, who related this parable of the Friend at midnight, waits to make us all importunate friends.

Therefore, let us give ourselves to be intercessors. Let us cry with importunity to God when we see people who need help, when the spirit of compassion stirs within us, when we feel our own powerlessness to help, or when we see obstacles in the way of our getting an answer. God alone can help. And in answer to our prayer, He *will* help. In addition, we should do our utmost to train the next generation of Christians in what we have learned. Let us teach those who come after us how to enter the good land—the blessed life of unceasing prayer. Moses could not enter the land of Canaan, but there was one thing he could do—he could, at God's bidding, "charge Joshua, and encourage him, and strengthen him" (Deuteronomy 3:28).

The model intercessor is the model Christian worker. The secret of successful work is to give away daily what we ourselves are receiving from God. Intercession is the blessed link between our impotence and God's omnipotence.

Chapter 4

BECAUSE OF HIS IMPORTUNITY

"I say unto you, Though he will not rise and give him, because he is his friend, yet because of his importunity he will rise and give him as many as he needeth"—Luke 11:8.

"And He spake a parable unto them to this end, that men ought always to pray, and not to faint. . . . Hear what the unjust judge saith. And shall not God avenge His own elect, which cry day and night unto Him, though he bear long with them? I tell you that He will avenge them speedily"—Luke 18:1-8.

Our Lord Jesus thought it was so important for us to realize the need for perseverance and importunity in prayer, that He gave us two parables to teach us this. That should prove that in such persevering and importuning we have, at once, prayer's greatest difficulty and its highest power. Christ wants us to know that prayer will not always be easy and smooth. We must expect difficulties, which can only be conquered by determined persistence.

In the parables, our Lord presents the difficulty

as belonging to the persons to whom the petition was addressed, and the importunity as needed to overcome their reluctance to hear. In our communion with God, the difficulty is not on His side, but on ours. In connection with the first parable, He tells us that our Father is more willing to give good things to those who ask Him than any earthly father would be to give his child bread. In the second, He assures us that God longs to avenge His elect speedily. The need of urgent prayer cannot be because God must be made willing or disposed to bless; the need lies altogether in ourselves. But because it was not possible to find any earthly illustration of a loving father or a willing friend from whom the needed lesson of importunity could be taught, He takes the unwilling friend and the unjust judge to instill in us the faith that perseverance in prayer can overcome every obstacle.

The difficulty is not in God's love or power, but in ourselves and our own incapacity to receive the blessing. And yet, because of this difficulty—our lack of spiritual preparedness—God has difficulty, too. His wisdom and His righteousness—indeed His love—dare not give us what would do us harm if we received it too soon or too easily. The sin, or the consequences of sin, that makes it impossible for God to answer immediately is a barrier on God's side as well as on ours. To break through this power of sin in ourselves, or in those for whom we pray, is what makes the striving and the conflict of prayer such a reality. Men of all ages have prayed (quite correctly) with the sense that there were difficulties in the heavenly world to overcome. As they pleaded with God for the removal of the unknown obstacles, and in that persevering supplication were brought into a state of utter brokenness and helplessness, they became entirely resigned to Him, in union with His will, with the faith that could take hold of Him. Then, the hindrance in themselves and in heaven were together overcome. As God conquered them, they conquered God. As God prevails over us, we prevail with God.

God has created us in such a way that, the clearer our insight into the reasonableness of a demand, the heartier our surrender to it. One great cause of our remissness in prayer is that there appears to be something arbitrary, or at least something incomprehensible, in the call to such continued prayer. If we could be brought to see that this apparent difficulty is a Divine necessity, and the source of unspeakable blessing, we would be ready to give ourselves with gladness of heart to persevering prayer. Let us attempt to understand how the difficulty that the call to importunity presents is one of our greatest privileges.

I do not know whether you have ever noticed what part difficulties play in our natural life. They call out man's powers as nothing else can. They strengthen and ennoble character. What is education, for example, but a daily developing and disciplining of the mind as increasingly difficult problems are presented to the pupil to be overcome?

The moment a lesson has become easy, the pupil is moved on to one that is more advanced. In the meeting and the mastering of difficulties, our highest attainments are to be found.

It is the same in our relationship with God. Just imagine what the result would be if the child of God had only to ask and receive and go away. What unspeakable loss to the spiritual life would result! Difficulty and delay require persevering prayer to obtain the true blessing and blessedness of the heavenly life. As we persevere, we learn how little we delight in fellowshipping with God, and how little living faith we have in Him. We discover how earthly and unspiritual our heart still is, how little we have of God's Holy Spirit. We come to know our own weakness and unworthiness. We yield to God's Spirit to pray in us and to take our place in Christ Jesus, and we abide in Him as our only plea with the Father. There, our own will, strength, and goodness are crucified. There, we rise in Christ to newness of life, with our whole will dependent on God and His glory. Do let us begin to praise God for the need and the difficulty of importunate prayer. They are one of His choicest means of grace.

Consider what our Lord Jesus owed to the difficulties in His path. In Gethsemane, it was as if the Father chose not to hear. Jesus prayed even more earnestly, until "He was heard." In the way He opened up for us, He learned obedience by the things He suffered, and so was made perfect. His will was given up to God; His faith in God was tried and strengthened; the prince of this world, with all his temptations, was overcome. This is the new and living way He consecrated for us. It is in persevering prayer that we walk with and are made partakers of His very Spirit. Prayer is a form of crucifixion, of our fellowship with Christ's cross, of our giving up our flesh to the death. O Christians! Shouldn't we be ashamed of our reluctance to sacrifice the flesh, our own will, and the world, as evidenced in our reluctance to pray much? Can we learn the lesson which both nature and Christ teach? The difficulty of importunate prayer is our highest privilege; to overcome it will bring us our richest blessings.

There are various elements of importunity. The most important are perseverance, determination, and intensity. Beginning with the refusal to at once accept a denial, importunity grows to the determination to persevere, to spare no time or trouble, until an answer comes. It then rises to the intensity in which the whole being is given to God in supplication, and the boldness comes to grasp God's strength. It can be quiet and restful at one time, and passionate and bold at another. It can take time and be patient, and then claim at once what it desires. No matter what its form, it always means and knows that God hears prayer and it will be heard.

Remember its wonderful appearances in the Old Testament. Think of Abraham, as he pleads for Sodom. Time after time, he renews his prayer, until the sixth time, he has to say, "Let not my Lord be angry" (Genesis 18:32). He does not cease until he has heard God's answer for each of his requests, until he has learned how far he can go, has entered into God's mind, and rests in God's will. For his sake, Lot was saved. "God remembered Abraham, and sent Lot out of the midst of the overthrow" (Genesis 19:29). Shouldn't we, who have redemption and promises for the unsaved which Abraham never knew, begin to plead more with God on their behalf?

Think of Jacob, when he feared meeting Esau. The angel of the Lord met him in the dark and wrestled with him (Genesis 32:24-32). When the angel saw that he could not win, he said, "Let me go." And Jacob answered, "I will not let thee go, except thou bless me." The angel blessed him then and there. The boldness that said, "I will not let thee go," forcing the blessing from the reluctant angel, was so pleasing in God's sight that Jacob was given a new name: "Israel (he who striveth with God): for as a prince hast thou power with God and with men, and hast prevailed."

Through all the ages, God's children have understood what Christ's two parables teach: God holds Himself back, and tries to get away from us, until what is of flesh, self, and sloth in us is overcome and we so prevail with Him that He can and must bless us. Why do so few of God's children desire this honor—being princes of God, strivers with God who prevail? What our Lord taught us, "What things soever ye desire, . . . *believe that ye receive them*" (Mark 11:24), is nothing but His restatement of Jacob's words, "I will not let thee go, except thou bless me." This is the importunity He teaches, and we must learn to claim and take the blessing.

Think of Moses when Israel had made the golden calf. Moses returned to the Lord and said, "Oh, this people have sinned a great sin: . . . Yet now, if Thou wilt forgive their sin—; and if not, blot me, I pray thee, out of thy book which thou hast written" (Exodus 32:31-32). That was importunity—Moses would rather have died than not have his people given to him. When God heard him, He promised Moses that He would send His angel to go with the people. But Moses went to Him again, and would not be content until, in answer to his prayer, God promised He Himself would go with them (Genesis 33:12,17-18). He said, "I will do this thing that thou hast spoken." After that, when in answer to Moses' prayer, "Shew me Thy glory," God made His goodness pass before him, Moses once again began pleading, "Let my Lord, I pray Thee, go among us." And he was there with the Lord forty days and forty nights (Exodus 34:28). Of these days he says, "I fell down before the Lord, as at the first forty days and forty nights, I did neither eat bread, nor drink water, because of all your sin which ye sinned."

As an intercessor, Moses used importunity with God and prevailed. He proves that the man who truly lives near to God, and with whom God speaks face to face, becomes partaker of that same power of intercession which there is in Him who is at God's right hand and ever lives to pray.

Think of Elijah in his prayer, first for fire, and

then for rain. In the former, you have the importunity that claims and receives an immediate answer. In the latter, bowing himself down to the earth, his face between his knees, his answer to the servant who had gone to look toward the sea, and come with the message, "There is nothing," was "Go again" seven times. Here was the importunity of perseverance. He had told Ahab there would be rain. He knew it was coming; and yet he prayed until the seven times were fulfilled. Of Elijah and his prayers, we are taught, "Pray one for another...Elijah was a man subject to like passions as we are...The effectual fervent prayer of a righteous man availeth much" (James 5:16-17). Where is the Lord God of Elijah, this God who draws out such effectual prayer, and hears it so wonderfully? His Name be praised—He is still the same! Let His people simply believe that He still waits to be inquired of! Faith in a prayer-hearing God will make a prayer-loving Christian.

Remember the marks of the true intercessor, as the parable taught us: a sense of human need; a Christlike love in the heart; a consciousness of personal impotence; faith in the power of prayer; courage to persevere in spite of refusal; and the assurance of an abundant reward. These characteristics constitute a Christian intercessor, and release the power of prevailing prayer. They constitute the beauty and the health of Christian life, fitting a man for being a blessing in the world, and making him a true Christian worker, who does, indeed, get from

God the bread of heaven to dispense to the hungry. These dispositions elicit the highest—the heroic—virtues of the life of faith.

There is nothing to which the nobility of natural character owes so much as it does to the spirit of enterprise and daring, which in travel, war, politics, or science, battles with difficulties and conquers. No labor or expense is too great for the sake of victory. Shouldn't we Christians be able to face difficulties through prayer? As we "labour" and "strive" in prayer, our renewed will asserts its royal right to claim, in the Name of Christ, what it will, wielding its God-given power to influence the destinies of men. Shouldn't men of the world sacrifice ease and pleasure in their pursuits to fight their way through to the place where they find liberty for the captive and salvation for the perishing?

Let each servant of Christ learn to know his calling. His King ever lives to pray. The Spirit of the King ever lives in us to pray. The blessings which the world needs must be called down from heaven in persevering, importunate, believing prayer. It is from heaven, in answer to such prayer, that the Holy Spirit will take complete possession of us to do His work through us. Let us acknowledge how vain all of our own work has been, due to our meager prayer. Let us change our method, so that more prayer, much prayer, unceasing prayer, is the proof that we look to God for everything, and that we believe that He hears us.

Chapter 5

THE LIFE THAT CAN PRAY

"If ye abide in Me, and My words abide in you, ye shall ask what ye will, and it shall be done unto you"—John 15:7.

"The effectual fervent prayer of a righteous man availeth much"—James 5:16.

"Beloved, if our heart condemn us not, then we have confidence toward God. And whatsoever we ask, we receive of Him, because we keep His commandments, and do those things that are pleasing in His sight"—1 John 3:21-22.

Here on earth, the success of someone asking a favor for others depends entirely on his character, and the relationship he bears to the person for whom he is interceding. What he is gives weight to what he asks. It is no different with God. Our power in prayer depends on our life. Where our life is right we will know to pray so as to please God, and prayer will secure the answer. The scriptures quoted above all point in this direction. *"If ye abide in Me,"* our Lord says, you shall ask, and it shall be done unto

48

you. It is the prayer of a *righteous man*, according to James, that avails much. We receive whatsoever we ask, John says, *because* we obey and please God. All lack of power to pray correctly and perseveringly, all lack of power in prayer with God, indicates some lack in the Christian life. As we learn to live the life that pleases God, God will give us what we ask for. Let us learn from our Lord Jesus, in the parable of the vine, what the healthy, vigorous, Christian life is, and how it may ask and receive whatever it desires. Hear His voice, "If ye abide in Me, and My words abide in you, ye shall ask what ye will, and it shall be done unto you." And again at the close of the parable: "Ye have not chosen Me, but I have chosen you, and ordained you, that ye should go and bring forth fruit, and that your fruit should remain: that *whatsoever ye shall ask* of the Father in My name, *He may give it you"* (John 15:16).

What sort of life is it, according to the parable, that we must lead to bear fruit, and then to ask and receive whatever we desire? What must we be or do, that will enable us to pray as we should, and to receive what we ask for? The answer is in one word: the branch-life gives power for prayer. We are branches of Christ, the Living Vine. We must simply live like branches—abide in Christ—then we shall ask what we will, and it shall be done unto us.

We all know what a branch is. Its essential characteristic is that it is simply a growth of the vine, produced by it and appointed to bear its fruit. It has only one reason for existence: it is there at the bidding of the vine, that through it the vine may bear and ripen its precious fruit. Just as the vine lives solely and wholly to produce the sap that makes the grape, so the branch has the singular object of receiving that sap and bearing the grape. Its only work is to serve the vine, in order that through it the vine may do its work.

Is the believer—the branch of Christ, the Heavenly Vine—as literally, as exclusively, to live only that Christ may bear fruit through him? Is a true Christian, as a branch, to be just as absorbed in and devoted to the work of bearing fruit to the glory of God as Christ the Vine was on earth, and is now in heaven? This, and nothing less, is indeed what is meant. It is to this branch-life that the unlimited prayer-promises of the parable are given. It is this branch-life—existing solely for the Vine—that will have the power to pray properly. When we abide in Him, and His words abide—kept and obeyed—in our heart and life, and are absorbed into our very being, then we will have the grace to pray correctly and the faith to receive the answer.

Do let us take Christ's two words, *anything* and *whatsoever*, and accept them in their simple, literal truth and their infinite, Divine grandeur. They are wonderfully repeated six times in the promises of our Lord's farewell discourse (John 14:13-14; 15:7,16; 16:23-24). Because they appear altogether too large for us to take them literally, we qualify them to meet our human ideas of what appears right. This is because we separate them from that life of absolute and unlimited devotion to Christ's service to which they were given.

God's covenant is always: Give all and take all. Whoever is willing to be wholly branch, and nothing but branch, must be ready to place himself absolutely at the disposal of Jesus, the Vine of God, to bear His fruit, and to live every moment only for Him. This person will receive a Divine liberty to claim Christ's *whatsoever* in all its fullness, and a Divine wisdom and humility to use it right. He will live and pray, claiming the Father's promises as Christ did, only for God's glory in the salvation of men. He will use his boldness in prayer only for power in intercession and getting men blessed. The unlimited devotion of the branch-life to fruit-bearing and the unlimited access to the treasures of the Vine-life are inseparable. It is only the life abiding wholly in Christ that can pray the effective prayer in the Name of Christ.

Think, for a moment, of the men of prayer in Scripture, and see in them the life that could pray in such power. We spoke of Abraham as an intercessor. What gave him such boldness? He knew that God had chosen and called him away from his home and people to walk before Him, that all nations might be blessed in him. He knew that he had obeyed and forsaken everything for God. Implicit obedience, to the very sacrifice of his son, was the law of his life. He did what God asked of him: he dared to trust God to do whatever he asked. We spoke of Moses as an intercessor. He, too, had forsaken everything for God, "esteeming the reproach of Christ greater riches than the treasures in Egypt" (Hebrews 11:26). He lived at God's disposal: "he was faithful in all His house as a servant" (Hebrews 3:5). How often it is written of him: "According to all that the Lord commanded Moses, so did he" (Exodus 40:16). No wonder he was so very bold. His heart was right with God, and he knew God would hear him. This is no less true of Elijah, the man who took his stand for the Lord God of Israel. The man who is ready to risk everything for God, can count on God to do everything for him.

Men pray as they live, because it is the life that prays. The life that, with wholehearted devotion, gives up everything for God and to God, can claim everything from God. Our God longs exceedingly to prove Himself the Faithful God and Mighty Helper of His people. He only waits for hearts that are completely turned from the world to Himself, and are open to receive His gifts. The man who loses all will find all; he will dare to ask and, then, take it. The branch that only and truly lives abiding in Christ, the Heavenly Vine, the branch that is entirely given up, like Christ, to bear fruit in the salvation of men, the branch that has Christ's words taken into and abiding in its life, may and dare ask what it will; it will be done. We may not yet have attained that full devotion to which our Lord had trained His disciples, neither may we equal them in their power of prayer. We may, nevertheless, take courage in remembering that every new step we take in our

Christian life toward the perfect branch-life, and every surrender to live for others in intercession, will be met from above by a corresponding liberty to pray with greater boldness and expect larger answers. The more we pray, and the more conscious we become of our unfitness to pray in power, the more we will be urged and helped to press on toward the key to power in prayer—a life abiding in Christ, entirely at His disposal.

Is there anyone concerned about why they have failed to attain this blessed branch-life, so simple and yet so mighty? Do they wonder how to reach it? Let me point them to one of the most precious lessons of the parable of the Vine, one that is all too little noticed. Jesus said, "I am the true Vine, *and my Father is the Husbandman.*" It is, indeed, something very wonderful that we have Christ, the glorified Son of God, whose Divine fullness of life and grace we can share. But there is something more wonderful still. We have the Father, as the Husbandman, watching over our abiding in the Vine, over our growth and fruit-bearing. It is not left to our faith or our faithfulness to maintain our union with Christ. God—the Father of Christ, who united us with Him—will see to it that the branch is what it should be. He will enable us to bring forth just the fruit we were appointed to bear. Hear what Christ said of this: "Every branch that beareth fruit, He purgeth it, that it may bring forth more fruit" (John 15:2). More fruit is what the Father seeks; more fruit is what the Father Himself will provide. It is for this that He, as

53

the Vinedresser, cleanses the branches.

Think for a moment what this means. It is said that of all fruit-bearing plants on earth, there is none that produces fruit so full of spirit—from which spirit can be so abundantly distilled—as the vine. And of all fruit-bearing plants, there is none that is so prone to overgrowth, and for which pruning and cleansing are so indispensable. The one great work that a vinedresser must do for the branch every year is to prune it. Other plants can, for a time, bear fruit without pruning. But the vine *must* have it. Therefore, the branch that desires to abide in Christ and bring forth much fruit—that desires to be able to ask whatsoever it will—must trust in and yield to the Divine cleansing.

What exactly does the vinedresser cut away with his pruning knife? Nothing but the wood that the branch has produced; true, honest wood, with the vine's true nature in it. This must be cut away. And why? Because it draws away the strength and life of the vine, and hinders the flow of the juice to the grape. The more it is cut down, the less wood there is in the branch, and the more sap that goes to the grape. The wood of the branch must decrease, that the fruit for the vine may increase. In obedience to the law of all nature, death is the way to life and gain comes through sacrifice. The rich and luxuriant growth of wood must be cut off and discarded in order that more abundant life may be seen in the cluster.

Child of God, branch of the Heavenly Vine,

there is a part of you which may appear perfectly innocent and legitimate, but it depletes your interest and your strength to such an extent that it must be pruned and cleansed away. We know what power in prayer men like Abraham, Moses, and Elijah had, and we know what fruit they bore. But how often do we remember what it cost them?—how God had to separate them from their surroundings and repeatedly draw them from trusting in themselves, so they would seek their life in Him alone. We will bear much fruit only when our own will, strength, effort, and pleasure (even where these appear perfectly natural and sinless) are cut down, leaving our entire being free and open to receive the sap of the Heavenly Vine, the Holy Spirit. It is in the surrender of what human nature holds fast in the full and willing submission to God's holy pruning knife—that we will become what Christ chose and appointed us for: fruit-bearers, to whom whatever is requested from the Father in Christ's name, will be given.

Christ tells us in the next verse what the pruning knife is: "Ye are *clean through the word* which I have spoken unto you" (John 15:3). As He says later, "Sanctify them through Thy truth; Thy word is truth" (John 17:17). "The word of God is sharper than any two-edged sword, piercing even to the dividing asunder of soul and spirit" (Hebrews 4:12). Christ had spoken such heart-searching words to His disciples on love and humility, being the least and, like Himself, the servant of all, denying self, taking the cross, and losing the life. Through His

Word, the Father had cleansed them, cutting away all confidence in themselves or the world, preparing them for the inflowing and filling of the Spirit of the Heavenly Vine. We cannot cleanse ourselves; God is the Vinedresser. We may confidently entrust ourselves to His care.

Beloved brethren—ministers, missionaries, teachers, workers, believers old and young—are you mourning your lack of prayer and, as a consequence, your lack of power in prayer? O come and listen to your beloved Lord as He tells you to be a branch, united to and identified with the Heavenly Vine; your prayers will then be effective and powerful. Are you despairing because you do not, you cannot, live this branch-life, abiding in Him? Come and listen again. For you to bear "more fruit" is not only your desire, but the Father's, too. He is the Husbandman who cleanses the fruitful branch, so it can bear more fruit. Cast yourself upon God to do in you what is impossible for man. Count upon a Divine cleansing to cut down and take away all that self-confidence and self-effort that has been the cause of your failure. The God who gave you His beloved Son to be your Vine, who made you His branch, will do His work of cleansing to make you fruitful in every good work, including the work of prayer and intercession.

The life that can pray is a branch entirely given up to the Vine and the Vine-life. All responsibility for its cleansing is cast on the Vinedresser. A branch abiding in Christ, trusting and yielding to God for His cleansing, can bear much fruit. In the power of such a life we will love prayer; we will know how to pray; we will pray and receive whatsoever we ask.

Chapter 6

IS RESTRAINING PRAYER SIN?

"Thou...restrainest prayer before God" — Job 15:4.

"What profit should we have, if we pray unto Him?"—Job 21:15.

"God forbid that I should sin against the Lord in ceasing to pray for you"—1 Samuel 12:23.

"Neither will I be with you any more, except ye destroy the accursed from among you"—Joshua 7:12.

Any deep quickening of the spiritual life of the Church will always be accompanied by a deeper sense of sin. This will not be caused by theology, which can only give expression to what God has already worked in the life of His people. Nor will this deeper sense of sin only be seen in stronger expressions of self-reproach, which often consist of the harboring of sin and unbelief. But the true sense of the hatefulness of sin and the hatred of it will be proved by the intensity of desire for deliverance and the struggle to know to the very utmost what God's power to save is. It is no less than a holy jealousy, to sin against God in nothing.

If we are to deal effectively with the lack of prayer, we must look at it from this point of view and ask, "Is restraining prayer a sin?" And if it is, how should it be discovered, confessed, cast out by man, and cleansed away by God? Jesus is a Savior from sin. Only when we truly know sin can we truly know the power that saves from sin. The life that can pray effectively is the life of the cleansed branch—the life that knows deliverance from the power of self. To see that our prayer-sins are indeed sins is the first step to a true and Divine deliverance from them.

In the story of Achan (Joshua 7), we have one of the strongest proofs in Scripture that it is sin which robs God's people of His blessing, and that God will not tolerate it. It is, at the same time, the clearest indication of the principles under which God deals with sin and removes it. Let us see, in the light of the story, if we can learn how to look at the sin of prayerlessness, and at the sinfulness that lies at the root of it. The words I have quoted above, "neither will I be with you any more, except ye put away the accursed thing from among you," take us into the very heart of the story. They suggest a series of precious lessons around the truth they express: the presence of sin makes the presence of God impossible.

1. *The presence of God is the great privilege of God's people, and their only power against the enemy.* God had promised to bring Moses into the

promised land. Moses proved that he understood this when, after the sin of the golden calf, God spoke of withdrawing His presence and sending an angel. Moses refused to accept anything less than God's presence. "For wherein shall it be known here that I and Thy people have found grace in Thy sight? Is it not in that *Thou goest with us?*" (Exodus 33:16). This gave Caleb and Joshua their confidence: the Lord is with us. This gave Israel their victory over Jericho: the presence of God. Throughout Scripture, this is the great, central promise: I am with thee. The wholehearted believer is separated from the worldling and worldly Christians around him by living consciously hidden in the secret of God's presence.

2. *Defeat and failure always result from the loss of God's presence.* It was thus at Ai. God had brought His people into Canaan with the promise to give them the land. When the defeat at Ai took place, Joshua felt at once that the cause must be in the withdrawal of God's power. He had not fought for them. His presence had been withheld.

In the Christian life and the work of the Church, defeat is always a sign of the loss of God's presence. If we apply this truth to our failure in the prayer life, considering our failure in work for God, we are led to see that it all simply goes back to our not standing in clear and full fellowship with God. His nearness, His immediate presence, has not been the chief thing sought after and trusted in. He could not work in us as He desired. Loss of blessing and power is always caused by the loss of God's presence.

3. *The loss of God's presence always results from some hidden sin.* Just as, in nature, pain is a warning sign of some hidden evil in the system, defeat is God's voice telling us there is something wrong. He has given Himself so wholly to His people, He delights so in being with them, and would so glady reveal His love and power in them, that He never withdraws unless He is compelled to do so by their sin.

The Church is complaining about many defeats today: she has so little power in the civilized world; the preaching of the Gospel everywhere is paralyzed by the scarcity of money and men; powerful conversions are rare; and the number of holy, consecrated, spiritual Christians, devoted to the service of God and their fellow-men is small. This all stems from a lack of the effective prayer which brings the Holy Spirit in power to ministers, believers, missionaries, and unsaved souls. Can we deny that our lack of prayer is the sin causing God's presence and power to be so far from us?

4. *God Himself will discover the hidden sin.* We may think we know what the sin is, but only God can discover its real and deep meaning. When He spoke to Joshua before naming the sin of Achan, God first said, "They have also transgressed My covenant which I commanded them" (Joshua 7:11). God had commanded (6:19) that all the booty of Jericho— gold, silver, and everything else—was to be consecrated unto the Lord, be placed in His treasury.

Israel had broken this consecration vow; it had not given God what was due Him; it had robbed God.

We need God to show us how our lack of prayer indicates an unfaithfulness to our consecration vow: to give God all of our heart and life. Our limited prayer, with the excuses we make for it, is a greater sin than we know. It shows that we have little taste or relish for fellowship with God; that our faith rests more on our own work and efforts than on the power of God. It demonstrates that we have little sense of the heavenly blessing God waits to shower down on us; that we are not ready to sacrifice the ease and confidence of the flesh for perseveringly waiting on God. And finally, it proves that the spirituality of our life—our abiding in Christ—is altogether too weak to make us prevail in prayer. When the pressure of work for Christ is allowed to be the excuse for our not finding time to seek and secure His own presence and power in it as our chief need, our sense of absolute dependence on God is not right. It shows we have no deep understanding of the Divine and supernatural work of God in which we are only His instruments, no true entrance into the heavenly, altogether other-worldly, character of our mission, and no full surrender to and delight in Christ Jesus Himself.

If we would allow God's Spirit to show us that all this comes from negligence in prayer, and of misplaced priorities, all our excuses would fall away. We would fall down and cry, "We have sinned! We have sinned!" Samuel once said, "As for me, God forbid that I should sin against the Lord in ceasing to pray for you" (1 Samuel 12:23). Ceasing from prayer is sin against God. May God reveal this to us.

5. *When God reveals sin, it must be confessed and cast out.* When the defeat at Ai came, Joshua and Israel were ignorant of the cause. Because God dealt with Israel as a nation—as one body—they were all held accountable for the sin of one member. Israel as a whole was unaware of the sin, and yet suffered for it. The Church may be unaware of the greatness of the sin of limited prayer, individual ministers or believers may never have considered it an actual transgression, but it nevertheless brings punishment. When the Holy Spirit begins to convict us of it, and the sin is no more hidden, then the time of heart-searching begins. In our story, the combination of individual and united responsibility is very solemn. As for the individual, God took each one, "man by man." Every man felt himself under the eye of God, to be dealt with, and when Achan had been taken, he had to make confession. As for the united body, all Israel suffered as God dealt with them. Then, together, "all Israel" stoned and burned Achan, his family, and "the accursed" out of their midst.

If we have reason to think that our lack of prayer is the sin in our camp, let us first confess it, both personally and unitedly. Then, let us come before God to destroy and put away the sin. The heap of stones in the valley of Achor stands at the very threshold of Israel's history in Canaan, to remind us that God cannot bear sin, that God will not dwell with sin, and that, *if we really want God's presence in power, sin must be put away*. The solemn fact is this: although there may be many other sins, to not pray as Christ and Scripture teach us is definitely one that causes the loss of God's presence. We must bring this sin out before God and give it up to the death. Then we must yield ourselves to God and obey His voice. No fear of past failure, no threatening array of temptations, duties, or excuses must keep us back. It is a simple question of obedience.

Are we going to give ourselves up to God and His Spirit, to live a life in prayer which is pleasing to Him? Surely—if God truly has been withholding His presence from us, if He really has been revealing our sin, if He really is calling for its destruction and our return to obedience—surely we can depend on His grace to accept and strengthen us for the life He desires of us. It is not a question of what you can do. It is a question of whether, with your whole heart, you give God what is due Him, surrendering yourself to let His will and grace have their way with you.

6. *With sin cast out, God's presence is restored.* From this day onward, there is not a word in the book of Joshua of defeat in battle. The story shows them going on from victory to victory. The securing of God's presence gives power to overcome every enemy.

This truth is so simple that the very ease with which we acquiesce to it robs it of its power. Let us pause and think about what it implies. If, when God is with us, we are victorious, then the responsibility for defeat must lie in our hands. This means that some sin must be causing it. Therefore, we should immediately search out and put away that sin. We may confidently expect God's presence the moment this is done. But each of us has a solemn obligation to examine his life to find what part he may have in this evil.

God never speaks to His people about sin except with the purpose of saving them from it. *The same light that shows the sin will show the way out of it.* The same power that breaks down and condemns, if humbly yielded to and waited on in confession and faith, will make it possible to rise up and conquer. It is God who is speaking to His Church and to us about this sin: "*He ... wondered* that there was no intercessor"; "*I wondered ...* that there was none to uphold"; "*I sought* for a man ... that should ...stand in the gap before Me, and found none" (Isaiah 59:16; 63:5; Ezekiel 22:30). The God who speaks thus will work this change for His children who seek His face: He will make the valley of Achor—of trouble and shame, of sin confessed and cast out—a door of hope. Let us not fear nor cling to the excuses and explanations which circumstances suggest. All we must do is to simply confess, "We have sinned; we are sinning; we dare not sin any longer." God does not demand impossibilities of us in prayer. He does not weary us with an impractical ideal. He asks us to pray no more than what He gives us grace to do. We may, therefore, rest assured that

He will give us the grace to pray so that our intercessions will be a pleasure to Him and to us, a source of strength to our conscience and our work, and a channel of blessing to those for whom we labor.

God dealt personally with Joshua, with Israel, and with Achan. Let each of us allow Him to deal personally with us concerning this sin of too little prayer, its consequences in our life and work, the deliverance from sin, and its certainty and blessedness. Just bow in stillness and wait before God until He overshadows you with His presence. Let Him lead you out of the region of human reasoning, where conviction of sin can never be deep, and full deliverance can never come. Take quiet time and be still before God, so that He may take this matter in hand. "Sit still, . . . for He will not be in rest until He have finished this thing this day." Leave yourself in God's hands.

Chapter 7

WHO SHALL DELIVER?

"Is there no balm in Gilead; is there no physician there? why then is not the health of the daughter of my people recovered?"—Jeremiah 8:22.

"Return, ye backsliding children, and I will heal your backslidings. Behold, we come unto Thee; for Thou art the Lord our God"—Jeremiah 3:22.

"Heal me, O Lord, and I shall be healed"—Jeremiah 17:14.

"Wretched man that I am! who shall deliver me from the body of this death? I thank God through Jesus Christ our Lord.... The law of the Spirit of life in Christ Jesus hath made me free from the law of sin and death"—Romans 7:24-25; 8:2.

A gentlemen once came to me for advice and help. He was evidently an earnest and well-instructed Christian man. For several years, he had been in quite difficult surroundings, trying to witness for Christ. The result was a sense of failure and unhappiness. His complaint was that he had no relish for the Word, and that, though he prayed, it was as if his heart was not in it. If he spoke to others, or gave a tract, it was under a sense of duty; the love and the joy were not present. He longed to be filled with God's Spirit, but the more he sought it, the farther off it appeared to be. What was he to think of his state, and was there any way out of it?

My answer was that the whole matter appeared to be very simple: he was living under the law and not under grace. As long as he did so, there could be no change. He listened attentively, but could not see exactly what I meant.

I reminded him of the difference, the absolute contrast between law and grace. Law demands; grace bestows. Law commands, but gives no strength to obey. Grace promises and performs, doing everything for us. Law burdens, casts down, and condemns. Grace comforts, makes strong and glad. Law appeals to self to do its utmost; grace points to Christ to do all. Law requires effort and strain, urging us toward a goal we can never reach. Grace works all of God's blessed will in us. I pointed out to him how his first step should be to completely accept his failure and his inability, as God had been trying to show him, instead of striving against it. With this acceptance and confession, he could sink down before God in utter helplessness. There he would learn that, unless grace gave him deliverance and strength, he could never do better than he had done, and that grace would, indeed, work all for him. He must come out from under law, self, and effort, taking his place under grace and allowing God to do all.

In later conversations he told me the diagnosis of the disease had been correct. He admitted grace must do everything. And yet, he had such a deep belief that he must do something, at least to be faithful, to secure the work of grace, that he feared his life would not change very much. He thought he would not be strong enough to handle the strain of new difficulties into which he was now going. There was, amid all his intense earnestness, an undertone of despair. He could not live as he knew he ought to.

I have already mentioned that I had noticed this tone of hopelessness. Every minister who has come into close contact with souls seeking to live wholly for God—to "walk worthy of the Lord unto all pleasing" (Colossians 1:10)—knows that this renders true progress impossible. There are many difficulties to be met, especially if one desires a fuller prayer life. We so often resolve to pray more and better, and then fail. We do not all have the strength of will required to change our habits. The pressure of duty is great. It is so difficult to find time for more prayer. We do not always feel real enjoyment in prayer, which would enable us to persevere. We do not have the necessary power for supplication and pleading, as we should. Instead of being a joy and a strength, our prayers are a source of continual self-condemnation and doubt. We have, at times, mourned and confessed and resolved. But, to tell the honest truth, we do not expect—for we do not see the way to—any great change.

It is evident that as long as this spirit prevails, there can be very little prospect of improvement. Discouragement must bring defeat. One of the first objects of a physician is to awaken and maintain hope. Without this, he knows his medicines will often accomplish little. No teaching from God's Word as to the duty, the urgent need, or the blessed privilege of more prayer will avail, as long as something lingers inside us whispering, "There is no hope." First, we must find the hidden cause of our failure and despair, and, then, realize how Divinely sure deliverance is. We must, unless we are to rest content with our state, listen to and join in the question, "Is there no balm in Gilead; is there no physician there? why then is not the health of the daughter of my people recovered?" We must listen to, and receive into our heart, the Divine promise: "Return, ye backsliding children, and I will heal your backsliding," and Israel's response: "Behold, we come unto Thee: for Thou art the Lord our God." We must come with the personal prayer, and have faith that there will be a personal answer. Let us begin now to claim it in regard to the lack of prayer, believing that God will help us: "Heal me, O Lord, and I shall be healed."

It is always important to distinguish between the symptoms of a disease and the disease itself. Weakness and failure in prayer is a sign of weakness in the spiritual life. If a patient were to ask a physician to give him something to stimulate his weak pulse, he would be told that this would do him little good. The pulse is the index of the state of the heart and the whole system. The physician is striving to have health restored. Everyone who would like to pray more faithfully and effectively must learn that his whole spiritual life is in a sickly state and needs restoration. His shortcoming in prayer is merely the symptom of his weak life of faith. Only when he realizes this will he become fully alive to the serious nature of the disease. He will then see the need for a radical change in his whole life and walk, if his prayer life—the pulse of his spiritual system—is to indicate health and vigor. God has created us in such a way that the exercise of every healthy function causes joy. Prayer is meant to be as simple and natural as breathing or working are to a healthy man. The reluctance we feel, and the failure we confess, are God's own voice calling us to acknowledge our disease, and to come to Him for the healing He has promised.

And what is the disease of which the lack of prayer is the symptom? We cannot find a better answer than is pointed out in the words, "Ye are not under the law, but under grace" (Romans 6:14).

This suggests the possibility of two types of Christian life: a life partly under the law and partly under grace, and a life entirely under grace, in the full liberty from self-effort and the full experience of the Divine strength which it can give. A true believer may still be living partly under the law, in the power of self-effort, striving to do what he cannot possibly accomplish. The continued failure in his Christian life results from his trusting in himself and trying to do his best. He does, indeed, pray and look to God for help, but it is still in his own strength, helped by God, that he does the work. In the Epistles to the Romans, the Corinthians, and the Galatians, Paul tells them that they have not received the spirit of bondage again; that they are free from the law; that they are no more servants, but sons; that they must beware of nothing so much as becoming entangled again with the yoke of bondage.

Everywhere in the New Testament we see this contrast between the law and grace, between the flesh, which is under the law, and the Spirit, who is the gift of grace, through whom grace does all its work. For us, just as for the early Church, the great danger is living under the law, serving God in the strength of our flesh. The great majority of Christians appear to remain in this state all their lives. This explains, to a large extent, their lack of true, holy living and power in prayer. They do not know that all failure can have but one cause: *Men seek to do themselves what grace alone can do in them,* what grace most certainly will do.

Many will not be prepared to admit that this is their disease, that they are not living "under grace." Impossible, they say. "From the depth of my heart," a Christian cries, "I believe and know that there is no good in me, and that I owe everything to grace alone." "I have spent my life," a minister says, "and found my glory in preaching and exalting the doctrines of free grace." "And, I," a missionary answers, "how could I ever have thought of seeing the heathen saved, if my only confidence had not been in the message I brought, and the power I trusted, of God's abounding grace." Surely you cannot say that our failures in prayer (and we sadly confess them) are caused by our not living under grace? This cannot be our disease.

We know it is possible for a man to be suffering from a disease without knowing it. What he believes to be a slight ailment turns out to be quite dangerous. Do not let us be too sure that we are not, to a large extent, still living "under the law," while considering ourselves to be living wholly "under grace." Very frequently, the reason for this mistake is the limited meaning attached to the word "grace." Just as we limit God Himself by our little or unbelieving thoughts of Him, so we limit His grace at the very moment we are delighting in terms like the "riches of grace" and "grace exceeding abundant." The very term, "grace abounding," has been confined to the one great, blessed truth of free justification with the ever-renewed pardon and eternal glory for the vilest of sinners. Yet, the equally blessed truth of "grace abounding" in sanctification is not fully known. Paul writes: "Much more they which receive abundance of grace...shall reign in life by one, Jesus Christ" (Romans 5:17). That reigning in life, as conquerors over sin, exists even here on earth. "Where sin abounded"—in the heart and life—"grace did much more abound: that grace reign through right-

73

eousness" in the whole life and being of the believer (Romans 5:20-21). It is of this reign of grace in the soul that Paul asks, "Shall we sin, because we are under grace?" and answers, "God forbid" (Romans 6:15). Grace is not only pardon of, but power over, sin. Grace takes the place sin had in the life, and undertakes, as sin had reigned within the power of death, to reign in the power of Christ's life. It is of this grace that Christ spoke, "My grace is sufficient for thee," and Paul answered, "I will glory in my infirmities...for when I am weak, then am I strong" (2 Corinthians 12:9-10). It is this grace which, when we are willing to confess ourselves utterly impotent and helpless, comes in to work all in us. It is of this grace that Paul teaches, "God is able to make *all grace* abound toward you; that ye, *always* having *all sufficiency* in *all things*, may abound to *every good work*" (2 Corinthians 9:8).

It often happens that a seeker of God and salvation will read his Bible much, and yet never see the truth of a free and full and immediate justification by faith. Once his eyes are opened and he accepts it, he is amazed to find it everywhere. In just the same way, many believers who believe in the doctrines of free grace as applied to pardon have never seen its wondrous meaning to work a whole new life in us. It can *actually give us strength every moment* for whatever the Father wills us to be and do. When God's light shines into our heart with this blessed truth, we know what Paul means, "Not I, but the grace of God." There again you have the twofold Christian life. One part is that in which the "Not I"—I am nothing, I can do nothing—has not yet become a reality. The other is when the wondrous exchange has been made, and grace has taken the place of our effort. Then we say and know, "I live; yet not I, but Christ liveth in me" (Galatians 2:20). This may then become a lifelong experience: "The grace of our Lord was exceeding abundant with faith and love which is in Christ Jesus" (1 Timothy 1:14).

Beloved child of God! do you believe it possible that this has been the problem in your life, the cause of your failure in prayer? You did not know how grace would enable you to pray, if you placed your whole life under its power. You sought by earnest effort to conquer your reluctance or deadness in prayer, but failed. You strove by every motive of shame or love you could think of to stir yourself to it, but it would not help. Wouldn't it be worth-while to ask the Lord whether the message I bring you as His servant may not be more true for you than you think? Your lack of prayer is the result of a diseased state of life, and the disease is this: you have not accepted, in your daily life and in your Christian duty, the full salvation which the Word brings. "Ye are not under the law, but under grace." The provision of grace and the power by which it makes us reign in life is not only as universal and deep-reaching as the demand of the law and the reign of sin, it is "more exceeding abundant."

In Romans 7, Paul gives us a picture of a believer's life under the law, with the bitter experience in which it ends: "O wretched man that I am! who shall deliver me from the body of this death?" His answer to the question, "I thank God through Jesus Christ our Lord," shows that there is deliverance from a life held captive by evil habits against which he struggled in vain. That deliverance is by the Holy Spirit giving us the full experience of what the life of Christ can work in us: "The law of the Spirit of life in Christ Jesus hath made me free from the law of sin and death" (Romans 8:2). The law of God could only deliver us into the bondage of the law of sin and death. The grace of God can bring us into, and keep us in, the liberty of the Spirit. We can be made free from the sad life under the power that held us captive and kept us from doing the righteous things we wanted to do. The Spirit of life in Christ can free us from our continual failure in prayer, and enable us to "walk worthy of the Lord unto all pleasing" (Colossians 1:10).

O do not be hopeless; do not be despondent! there is a balm in Gilead; there is a Physician there; there is healing for our sickness. What is impossible with man is possible with God. What you see no possibility of doing, grace will do. Confess the disease; trust the Physician; claim the healing; pray the prayer of faith: "Heal me, and I shall be healed." You too can become a man of prayer, and pray the effectual prayer that avails much.

Chapter 8

WILT THOU BE MADE WHOLE?

"Jesus saith unto him, Wilt thou be made whole? The impotent man answered him, Sir, I have no man...to put me into the pool...Jesus saith unto him, Rise...and walk. Immediately the man was made whole...and walked"—John 5:6-9.

"Peter said...In the name of Jesus Christ of Nazareth rise up and walk...The faith which is by Him hath given him this perfect soundness in the presence of you all"—Acts 3:6,16.

"Peter said...Eneas, Jesus Christ maketh thee whole: arise...And he arose immediately"—Acts 9:34.

Weakness in prayer is the mark of disease. The inability to walk is, in the Christian, as in the natural life, a terrible proof of some evil in the system that needs a physician. The lack of power to walk joyfully in the new and living way that leads to the Father and the throne of grace is especially grievous. Christ is the great Physician, who comes to every Bethseda where those who need healing are gathered, and asks

His loving, searching question, "Wilt thou be made whole?" For anyone still clinging to hope in the pool, or looking for some man to put him in, for anyone hoping somehow to be helped, in time, by just continuing in the use of the ordinary means of grace, His question points to a better way. He offers them healing in a way of power they have never understood. And to anyone willing to confess, not only his own powerlessness, but his failure to find any man to help him, His question brings the sure and certain hope of a near deliverance. We have seen that our weakness in prayer is part of a life afflicted with spiritual weakness. Let us listen to our Lord as He offers to restore our spiritual strength and to fit us for walking like healthy, strong men in all the ways of the Lord. Then we will be properly fit to take our place in the great work of intercession. As we see the wholeness He offers, how He gives it, and what He asks of us, we will be prepared for giving a willing answer to His question.

The Health that Jesus Offers

What are some of the marks of spiritual health? Our text leads us to one: walking. To the sick man Jesus said, "Rise and walk," and, with that, restored him to his place among men in full health and vigor, able to do his share of all the work of life. It is a wonderfully suggestive picture of the restoration of spiritual health. To the healthy, walking is a pleasure; to the sick, a burden, if not an impossibility. To many Christians, movement and progress in God's way is as wearying an effort as walking is to the lame. Christ comes to say, "Rise and walk," and with His word He gives the power to do so.

Think about this walk to which He restores and empowers us. It is a life like that of Enoch and Noah, who "walked with God" (Genesis 5:22; 6:9); a life like that of Abraham, to whom God said, "Walk before Me," and who himself said, "The Lord before whom I walk" (Genesis 17:1; 24:40); a life of which David sings, "They shall walk...in the light of Thy countenance" (Psalm 89:15), and Isaiah prophesies, "They that wait upon the Lord shall renew their strength;...they shall run, and not be weary; and they shall walk, and not faint" (Isaiah 40:31). Just as God the Creator does not faint nor become weary, they who walk with Him, waiting on Him, will never be exhausted or weak. Zacharias and Elisabeth, the last of the Old Testament saints, lived this life, and of them it was said "They were both righteous before God, walking in all the commandments and ordinances of the Lord blameless" (Luke 1:6). This is the walk Jesus came to make possible and true for His people in greater power than ever before.

Hear what the New Testament says of it: "That like as Christ was raised up from the dead by the glory of the Father, even so we should walk in newness of life" (Romans 6:4). It is the Risen One who says to us, "Rise and walk." He gives us the power of the resurrection life, which is a walk in Christ. "As ye have therefore received Christ Jesus the Lord, so walk ye in Him" (Colossians 2:6). It is a walk like Christ. "He that saith he abideth in Him ought himself also to walk, even as He walked" (1 John 2:6). It is a walk by the Spirit and after the Spirit. "Walk in the Spirit, and ye shall not fulfill the lust of the flesh" (Galatians 5:16). "Who walk not after the flesh, but after the Spirit" (Romans 8:1). It is a walk worthy of God and pleasing to Him. "That ye might walk worthy of the Lord, unto all pleasing, being fruitful in every good work" (Colossians 1:10). "I beseech you . . . that as ye have received of us how ye ought to walk and to please God, so ye would abound more and more" (1 Thessalonians 4:1). It is a walk in heavenly love. "Walk in love, as Christ also hath loved us" (Ephesians 5:2). It is a "walk in the light, as He is in the light" (1 John 1:7). It is a walk of faith, whose power comes simply from God and Christ and the Holy Spirit to the soul turned away from the world. "We walk by faith not by sight" (2 Corinthians 5:7). So many believers regard such a walk as impossible, so impossible that they do not feel it a sin that they "walk otherwise." Therefore, they do not long for this walk in newness of life. They have become so accustomed to the life of powerlessness that the life and walk in God's strength has little attraction. But there are some who are not like this. They wonder if these words really mean what they say, and if the wonderful life each one of them speaks of is simply an unattainable ideal, or meant to be realized in flesh and blood. The more they study them, the more they feel that they are spoken for daily life. And yet they appear too high. If only they would believe that God sent His Almighty Son and His Holy Spirit to *indeed* bring us and fit us for a life and walk from heaven beyond anything that man could dare to think or hope for.

How Jesus Makes Us Whole

When a physician heals a patient, he treats him externally and does something which, if possible, leaves his patient independent of his aid in the future. He restores him to perfect health, and leaves him. The work of our Lord Jesus is in both respects the very opposite. Jesus works not from without, but from within, by entering into our very life by the power of His Spirit. And instead of rendering the patient independent of His future assistance, Christ's one purpose in healing—His one condition of success—is to bring us into *such dependence on Him that we are not able to do without Him for one single moment*. Christ Jesus Himself *is* our life, in a sense that many Christians have no conception of.

Our prevailing weak and sickly life is entirely due to our lack of understanding of the Divine truth. As long as we expect Christ to perform single, occasional acts of grace for us from heaven, trusting Him each time to give us something that will last a little while, we cannot be restored to perfect health. But when we see how nothing is to be our own for a single moment, everything is supposed to be Christ, when we learn to accept this from Him and trust

Him for it, the life of Christ becomes the health of our soul. Health is nothing but life in its normal, undisturbed action. Christ gives us health by giving us Himself as our life. In this way, He becomes our strength for our walk. Isaiah's words find their New Testament fulfillment therein: They that wait on the Lord will walk and not faint, because Christ is now the strength of their life.

It is strange how believers sometimes think this life of dependence is too great a strain, and a loss of personal liberty. They admit a need of dependence, of much dependence, but with room left for their own will and energy. They do not see that even a partial dependence makes us debtors, and leaves us nothing to boast of. They forget that our relationship to God, and co-operation with Him, is not that He does the larger part and we the lesser, but that God does all and we do all—God all in us, we all through God. This dependence on God secures our true independence. When our will seeks nothing but the Divine will, we reach a Divine nobility, the true independence of all that is created. He who has not seen this must remain a sickly Christian, letting self do part and Christ part. He who accepts the life of unceasing dependence on Christ, as life and health and strength, is made whole. As God, Christ can enter into and become the life of His creature. As the Glorified One who received the Holy Spirit from the Father to bestow, He can renew the heart of the sinful creature and make it His home. By His presence, He can maintain it in full health and strength.

All of you who would rather walk and please God, so that in your prayer life, your heart does not condemn you, listen to Christ's words: "Wilt thou be made whole?" (John 5:6). He can give you soul-health. He can give you a life that can pray and know that it is pleasing the Father. If you desire this, come and hear how you can receive it.

What Christ Asks of Us

The story of the man at Bethseda invites us to notice three things very specially. Christ's question first appeals to the will, asking for the expression of its consent. He then listens to the man's confession of his utter helplessness. Then, comes the ready obedience to Christ's command, that rises up and walks.

1. The first step is, "Wilt thou be made whole?" There could be no doubt about the answer of the lame man. Who would not be willing to have his sickness removed? But, in the spiritual life there is a greater need to press the question. Some will not admit that they are so sick. Some will not believe that Christ can make a man whole. Some will believe it for others, but they are sure it is not for them. At the root of all this lies the fear of the self-denial and the sacrifice which will be needed. They are not willing to entirely forsake their walk in the world, to give up all self-will, self-confidence, and self-pleasing. The walk *in* Christ and *like* Christ is too straight and hard; they do not will it; they do not will

to be made whole. My brother and sister, if you are willing, speak it out: "Lord! at any price, I will!" It is Christ's will to make you clean and whole. But you must will it also. If you desire to be delivered from your sickness, say to Him without fear, "I will, I will!"

Then comes the second step. Christ wants us to look up to Him as our only Helper. "I have no man to put me in," must be our cry. Here on earth there is no help for me. Weakness may grow into strength in the ordinary way, if the body is in a sound state. But sickness requires special measures. Your soul is sick; your inability to walk the Christian walk joyfully is a sign of desease. Don't be afraid to confess it. Admit that there is no hope for restoration unless Christ's mercy heals you. Give up the idea of growing out of your sickly condition into a healthy one, of growing out from under the law into a life under grace. A few days ago, I heard a student say, "Do not think of 'growing into' a missionary. Unless God forbids you, take the step. The decision will bring joy and strength, will set you free to mature in everything needed to be a missionary, and will be a help to others." It is just the same in the Christian life. Delay and struggle will hinder you. Simply confess that you cannot bring yourself to pray as you should, because you cannot give yourself the healthy, heavenly life that loves to pray, that knows to count on God's Spirit to pray in us. Come to Christ to heal you. In one moment, He can make you whole. There may not be a sudden change in your feelings or in what you are in yourself. But, in heavenly reality, Christ will come in, in response to your surrender and faith, to take charge of your inner life and fill it with Himself and His Spirit.

The third thing Christ asks is the surrender of faith. When He spoke to the lame man, His command had to be obeyed. The man believed that there was truth and power in Christ's word; in that faith he rose and walked. By faith he obeyed. And what Christ said to others was for him, too: "Go thy way; thy faith hath made thee whole" (Mark 10:52). Christ asks this faith of us, too, in order for His word to change our sickness into strength, fitting us for that walk in newness of life for which we have been quickened in Him. If we do not believe this, if we will not take courage and say, with Paul, "I can do all things through Christ, which strengtheneth me" (Philippians 4:13), we cannot obey. But if we will listen to the word that describes the walk that is not only possible, but liveable, as proved by God's time-honored saints, if we fix our eye on the mighty, living, loving Christ, who speaks in power, "Rise and walk," we will take courage and obey. We will rise and begin to walk in Him and His strength. In faith, apart from and above all feeling, we will accept and trust an unseen Christ as our strength, and go on in the strength of the Lord God. We will know Christ as the strength of our life. We will know and tell and prove that Jesus Christ has made us whole.

Can it really happen? Yes, it can. He has done it for many; He will do it for you. Beware of forming wrong conceptions of what must take place. When the lame man was made whole, he still had to learn how to use his new-found strength. If he wanted to dig, build, or learn a trade, he had to begin at the beginning. Do not expect to be immediately proficient in prayer or any other part of the Christian life. But do expect and be confident of this one thing: because you have trusted yourself to Christ to be your health and strength, He will lead and teach you. Begin to pray in a quiet sense for your ignorance and weakness, but with a joyful assurance that He will work in you what you need. Rise and walk each day in a holy confidence that He is with you and in you. Just accept Jesus Christ the Living One, and trust Him to do His work.

Will you do it? Have you done it? Even now Jesus speaks, "Rise and walk." Answer Him: "Amen, Lord! At Your word I come. I rise to walk with You, in You, and like You."

Chapter 9

THE SECRET OF EFFECTUAL PRAYER

"What things soever ye desire, when ye pray, believe that ye received them, and ye shall have them"—Mark 11:24.

Here we have a summary of the teaching of our Lord Jesus on prayer. Nothing will convince us more of the sin of our negligence in prayer, revealing its causes and giving us courage to expect entire deliverance, than the careful study and believing acceptance of that teaching. The more heartily we enter into the mind of our blessed Lord, simply thinking about prayer as He thought, the more surely His words will become living seeds. They will grow and produce their fruit in us—a life corresponding exactly to the Divine truth they contain. Do let us believe this: Christ, the living Word of God, gives, in His words, a Divine quickening power which brings what they say, which works in us what He asks, and which actually enables us to do everything He demands. Learn to regard His teaching on prayer as a definite promise of what He, by His Holy Spirit dwelling in you, is going to work into your very being and character.

Our Lord gives us the five components, or essential elements, of true prayer. There must be, first, the heart's *desire*; then, the expression of that desire in *prayer*; with that, the *faith* that carries the prayer to God; in that faith, the *acceptance of God's answer*; then comes *the experience* of the desired blessing. It might help us to learn to pray believingly if we would each take a definite request to the Lord. Or, perhaps better still, we might all unite and take the one thing to Him that has been occupying our attention: our failure in prayer. We could take, as the object of our desire and supplication, the "grace of supplication." Together, we could ask and receive in faith the power to pray just as, and as much as, God expects of us. Let us meditate on our Lord's words, in the confidence that He will teach us how to pray for this blessing.

1. "What things soever *ye desire*." Desire is the secret power that moves the whole world of living men, and directs the course of each. It is, therefore, the soul of prayer. The cause of insufficient or unsuccessful prayer is very often found in the lack or weakness of desire. Some may doubt this; they are sure that they have very earnestly desired what they ask. But their desire may not be as wholehearted as God would have it, as the heavenly worth of these blessings demands. It may, indeed, be the lack of desire that is the cause of failure. What is true of God

is true of each of His blessings. And the more spiritual the blessing, the truer it is. "Ye shall seek Me, and shall find Me, when ye shall search for Me *with all your heart*" (Jeremiah 29:13).

Of Judah in the days of Asa it is written, "They sought Him with *their whole desire*" (2 Chronicles 15:15). A Christian may often have very earnest desires for spiritual blessings. But, besides these, there may be other desires in his daily life occupying a large place in his interests and affections. The spiritual desires are not all-absorbing. He wonders if his prayer is being heard. It is simply that God wants the whole heart. "The Lord our God is *one Lord*: and thou shalt love the Lord thy God with *all thy heart*" (Mark 12:29-30). The law is unchangeable: God offers Himself, gives Himself away, to the wholehearted who give themselves wholly away to Him. He always gives us according to our heart's desire, not as we think it, but as He sees it. If there are other desires which occupy our heart more than Himself and His presence, He allows these to be fulfilled, and the desires that engage us at the hour of prayer cannot be granted.

We desire the gift of intercession, grace, and power to pray correctly. Our hearts must be drawn away from other desires; we must give ourselves wholly to this one. We must be willing to live completely in intercession for the Kingdom. By fixing our eyes on the blessedness and the need of this grace, by believing with certainty that God will give it to us, by giving ourselves up to it for the sake of the perishing world, desire may be strengthened, and the first step taken toward the possession of the coveted blessing. Let us seek the grace of prayer, as we seek the God with whom it will link us, "with our whole desire." We can depend on the promise, "He will fulfill the desire of them that fear Him" (Psalm 145:19). Let us not be afraid to say to Him, "I desire it with my whole heart."

2. "What things soever ye desire when *ye pray*." The desire of the heart must become the expression of the lips. Our Lord Jesus more than once asked those who cried to Him for mercy, "What wilt thou?" He wanted them to say what they desired. To speak it out loud aroused their whole being into action. It brought them into contact with Him, and awakened their expectation. To pray is to enter into God's presence, to claim and secure His attention, to have distinct dealing with Him in regard to some request. Prayer is to commit our need to His faithfulness, and to leave it there. It is in so doing that we become fully conscious of what we are seeking.

There are some who often carry strong desires in their heart, without bringing them to God in the clear expression of definite and repeated prayer. There are others who go to the Word and its promises to strengthen their faith, but do not give sufficient attention to that pointed asking of God which helps to assure the soul that the matter has been put into God's hands. Still others come in prayer with so many requests and desires that it is difficult for them to say what they really expect God to do. If you desire from God this great gift of faithfulness in prayer and the power to pray properly, begin by exercising yourself in prayer about just that. Say to yourself and to God: "I would like to ask You for the grace of intercession. I am asking You for it now, and will continue to ask for it until I receive it. As plain and pointed as words can make it, I am saying, 'My Father! I do desire, I do ask of You, and I expect You to grant me this request.'"

3. "What things soever ye desire, when ye pray, *believe*." Because it is only by faith that we can know God, receive Jesus Christ, or live the Christian life, faith is the life and power of prayer. If we are to enter a life of intercession, in which there is joy and power and blessing, if we are to have our prayer for this grace of prayer answered, we must relearn what faith is. We must begin to live and pray in faith as never before.

Faith is the opposite of sight, and the two are contrary to each other. "We walk by faith, and not by sight." If the unseen is to get full possession of us, and our heart, life, and prayer are to be full of faith, there must be a withdrawal from, a denial of, the visible. The spirit that seeks to enjoy as much as possible that which is superficially innocent or legitimate, that gives the first place to the calls and duties of worldly life, is inconsistent with strong faith and close contact with the spiritual world. "We *look not* at the things which are seen"—the negative side needs to be emphasized if the positive, "but at the things which are not seen," is to become natural to us

(2 Corinthians 4:18). In praying, faith depends on our living in the invisible world.

This faith is especially important to knowing God. The great reason for our lack of faith is our lack of knowledge of God and our weak communication with Him. "Have faith in God," Jesus said when He spoke of removing mountains. Only as a soul comes to know God, becoming occupied with His power, love, and faithfulness, denying self and the world, and allowing the light of God to shine on it, will unbelief become impossible. All the mysteries and difficulties connected with answers to prayer will, however little we may be able to solve them intellectually, be swallowed up in the adoring assurance: "This God is our God. He will bless us. He does indeed answer prayer. And the grace to pray I am asking for He will delight to give."

4. "What things soever ye desire, when ye pray, believe that *ye have received*," now as you pray. Faith has to accept the answer, as given by God in heaven, before it is found or felt on earth. This point causes difficulty, and yet it is the very essence, the real secret, of believing prayer. Try and take it in. Spiritual things can only be spiritually understood or appropriated. The spiritual, heavenly blessing of God's answer to your prayer must be spiritually recognized and accepted before you feel anything of it. It is faith that accomplishes this. A soul that not only seeks an answer, but seeks first the God who gives the answer, receives the power to know that it has what it has asked of Him. If the soul knows that

it has asked according to His will and promises, that it has come to and found Himself to give it, then it does believe that it has received. "We know that He heareth us."

There is nothing as heart-searching as the faith, *"Believe that ye have received."* As we strive to believe and find we cannot, it leads us to discover what is hindering us. Blessed is the man who holds nothing back and lets nothing hold him back. With his eyes and heart on God alone, he refuses to rest until he has believed what our Lord bids him, "that he has received." Here is the place where Jacob becomes Israel, and the power of prevailing prayer is born out of human weakness and despair. Here is where the real need for persevering and importunate prayer comes in. It will not rest, go away, or give up, until it knows it is heard, and believes that it has received.

Are you praying for "the Spirit of grace and supplication"? Ask for it with a strong desire and believe in God who hears prayer. Do not be afraid to press on and believe that your life can indeed be changed, that the world, with its pressures and responsibilities that hinder prayer, can be overcome. Believe that God gives you your heart's desire and the grace to pray both in measure and in spirit, just as the Father would have His child do. "Believe that ye have received."

5. "What things soever ye desire when ye pray, believe that ye have received, and *ye shall have them.*" The receiving from God in faith—the believ-

ing acceptance of the answer with the perfect, praising assurance that it has been given—is not necessarily the experience or subjective possession of the gift we have asked for. At times, there may be a long interval of time between our asking and our actually receiving. In other cases, the believing supplicant may immediately experience the actual enjoyment of what he has received. It is especially in the former case that we need to have faith and patience: faith to rejoice in the assurance of the answer bestowed and received, and to begin acting on that answer even though nothing is felt; patience to wait if, for the present, there is no sensible proof of its reality. We can count on it: *Ye shall have*, in tangible reality.

If we apply this to the prayer for the power of faithful intercession—the grace to pray earnestly and perseveringly for souls around us—let us learn to grasp the Divine assurance that, as surely as we believe, we receive. Faith may, therefore, rejoice in the certainty of an answered prayer. The more we praise God for it, the sooner the experience will come. We may begin at once to pray for others, in the confidence that grace will be given us to pray more perseveringly and more believingly than we have ever done before. If we do not find any immediate growth or power in prayer, we must not be hindered or discouraged. We have accepted, apart from feeling, a spiritual, Divine gift by faith; in that faith we are to pray, doubting nothing. The Holy Spirit may, for a little time, be hiding Himself within us. But we can count on Him to pray in us, even though it is with groanings which cannot find expression. In due time, we will become conscious of His presence and power. As sure as there is desire, prayer, faith, and faith's acceptance of the gift, there will also be the manifestation and experience of the blessing we sought.

Beloved brethren! do you truly desire that God would enable you to pray in such a way that your life would be free from continual self-condemnation, and that the power of His Spirit would come down in answer to your petition? Come and *ask it of God*. Kneel down and pray for it in a single, definite sentence. When you have done so, remain kneeling in faith, believing in God who answers. Believe that you do now receive what you have prayed; believe that you have received. If you find it difficult to do this, remain kneeling and say that you are doing it on the strength of His own word. If it costs time, struggle, and doubt, fear not. While you are there at His feet, looking up into His face, faith will come. "Believe that you have received." At His bidding you dare to claim the answer. Begin a new prayer life in that faith, even though it may be weak. Let this one thought be its strength: you have asked and received grace in Christ to prepare you, step by step, to be faithful in prayer and intercession. The more simply you hold on to this and expect the Holy Spirit to work it in you, the more surely and fully this word will be made true to you: You will have it. God Himself who gave the answer will work it in you.

Chapter 10

THE SPIRIT OF SUPPLICATION

"I will pour upon the house of David...the Spirit of grace and of supplications"—Zechariah 12:10.

"The Spirit also helpeth our infirmities: for we know not what we should pray for as we ought: but the Spirit itself maketh intercession for us with groanings which cannot be uttered. And He that searcheth the hearts knoweth what is the mind of the Spirit, because He maketh intercession for the saints according to the will of God"—Romans 8:26-27.

"With all prayer and supplication in the Spirit, and watching thereunto with all perseverance and supplication for all the saints"—Ephesians 6:18.

"Praying in the Holy Spirit"—Jude 20.

The Holy Spirit has been given to every child of God to be his life. He dwells in him, not as a separate Being in one part of his nature, but as his very life. He is the Divine power or energy by which his life is maintained and strengthened. All that a believer is called to be or to do, the Holy Spirit can and will work in him. If he does not know or yield to the Holy Guest, the Blessed Spirit cannot work. His life will be a sickly one, full of failure and sin. As he yields, waits, and obeys the leading of the Spirit, God works in him everything that is pleasing in His sight.

The Holy Spirit is, in the first place, a Spirit of prayer. He was promised as a "Spirit of grace and supplication," the grace for supplication. He was sent forth into our hearts as "the Spirit of adoption, whereby we cry, Abba, Father" (Romans 8:15). He enables us to say, in true faith and growing understanding of its meaning, "Our Father which art in heaven." "He maketh intercession for the saints according to God." As we pray in the Spirit, our worship is as God desires it to be, "in spirit and in truth" (John 4:23). Prayer is the breathing of the Spirit in us. Power in prayer comes from the power of the Spirit in us, waited on and trusted in. Failure in prayer comes from the weakness of the Spirit's work in us. Our prayer is the index of the measure of the Spirit's work in us. For us to pray right, the life of the Spirit must be right in us. For praying the effective, prevailing prayer of the righteous man, everything depends on the indwelling of the Spirit.

There are three very simple lessons that the believer, who wants to enjoy the blessing of being taught to pray by the Spirit of prayer, must know.

The first is: *Believe that the Spirit dwells in you* (Ephesians 1:13). Deep in the inmost recesses of his being, hidden and unfelt, every child of God has the holy, mighty Spirit of God dwelling in him. He knows it by the faith that accepts God's promise and believes that of which he sees, as yet, no sign. "We receive the promise of the Spirit through faith" (Galatians 3:14). As long as we measure our prayer-power by what we feel or think we can accomplish, we will be discouraged when we hear how much we ought to pray. But when we quietly believe that, in the midst of all our weakness, the Holy Spirit as a Spirit of supplication is dwelling within us, *for the very purpose of enabling us to pray in the manner and measure that God desires*, our hearts will be filled with hope. We will be strengthened in the assurance which lies at the very root of a happy and fruitful Christian life—*God has made an abundant provision for our being what He wants us to be*. We will begin to lose our sense of burden, fear, and discouragement about our ever praying sufficiently, because we see that the Holy Spirit Himself will pray, is praying, in us.

The second lesson is: *Beware, above everything, of grieving the Holy Spirit* (Ephesians 4:30). If you do grieve Him, how can He work in you the quiet, trustful, and blessed sense of that union with Christ which makes your prayers pleasing to the Father? Beware of grieving Him by sin, by unbelief, by selfishness, and by unfaithfulness to His voice in conscience. Do not think that grieving Him is a necessity. That assumption cuts away the very sinews of your strength. Do not consider it impossible to obey the command, "Grieve not the Holy Spirit."

He Himself is the very power of God that makes it possible for you to be obedient. Your will can, in the power of the Spirit, at once reject any sin that rises up against your will, such as sloth, pride, self-will, or the passions of the flesh. Cast these on Christ and His blood, and your communion with God will be immediately restored. Each day, accept the Holy Spirit as your Leader and Life and Strength. You can depend on Him to make your heart everything it should be. There, in your heart, this Unseen and Unfelt One, who is known only by faith, provides the love, faith, and power of obedience you need. This is because He is revealing Christ, who is actually your Life and Strength, unseen within you. Do not grieve the Holy Spirit by distrusting Him just because you do not feel His presence in you.

Especially in the matter of prayer, do not grieve Him. When you trust Christ to bring you into a new, healthy prayer life, do not expect to be able, all at once, to pray as easily, powerfully, and joyfully as you would like to. No, it may not come all at once. But just bow quietly before God in your ignorance and weakness. The best and most sincere prayer comes when you put yourself before God just as you are, and count on the hidden Spirit praying in you. "We know not what to pray as we ought"; ignorance, difficulty, and struggle characterize our prayer all along. But, "the Spirit helpeth our infirmities." How? "The Spirit Himself," deeper down than our thoughts or feelings, "maketh intercession for us with groanings which cannot be uttered." When you cannot find words, when your words appear cold and powerless, just believe the Holy Spirit is praying in you. Be quiet before God; give Him time. In due season you will learn to pray. Beware of grieving the Spirit of prayer by not honoring Him in patient, trustful surrender to His intercession in you.

The third lesson: *"Be filled with the Spirit"* (Ephesians 5:18). We have seen the meaning of this great truth: It is only the healthy spiritual life that can pray right. The command comes to each of us: "Be filled with the Spirit." While some are content with a small measure of the Spirit's indwelling, it is God's will that we should be filled with the Spirit. That means that our whole being ought to be entirely yielded to the Holy Spirit, to be possessed and controlled by Him alone. We can count on and expect the Holy Spirit to take possession of and fill us. Our failure in prayer has been caused by our not having accepted the Spirit of prayer to be our life. We have not yielded wholly to Him, whom the Father gave as the Spirit of His Son, to work the life of the Son in us. Let us, to say the very least, be willing to receive Him, to yield ourselves to God, and to trust Him for it. Let us not again willfully grieve the Holy Spirit by declining, by neglecting, by hesitating to seek to have Him as fully as He is willing to give Himself to us. If we believe that prayer is the great need of our work and of the Church, if we truly desire to pray more, let us turn to the very source of all power and blessing. Let us believe that the Spirit of prayer, *in His fullness*, is for us.

We all know the place the Father and the Son have in our prayer. It is to the Father we pray, and from whom we expect the answer. It is in the merit, Name, and life of the Son, it is abiding in Him and He in us, that we trust we will be heard. But have we understood that in the Holy Trinity all Three Persons have an equal place in prayer, and that faith in the Holy Spirit of intercession is as indispensable as faith in the Father and the Son? How clearly this is stated in the words, "Through Him we have access by one Spirit to the Father" (Ephesians 2:18). As much as prayer must be *to* the Father, and *through* the Son, it must be *by* the Spirit. And the Spirit can pray in us only when He lives in us. It is only as we give ourselves to the Spirit living and praying in us, that the glory of the prayer-hearing God and the blessed mediation of the Son can be known by us in their power.

Our last lesson: *Pray in the Spirit for all saints* (Ephesians 6:18). The Spirit, who is called "the Spirit of supplication," is also the Spirit of intercession. It is said of Him: "the Spirit Himself maketh intercession for us with groanings that cannot be uttered." "He maketh intercession for the saints." Christ "also maketh intercession for us." The thought is essentially that of mediation—one pleading for another. When the Spirit of intercession takes full possession of us, all selfishness vanishes, and we no longer want to have Him for ourselves alone, apart from His intercession for others. We can begin to avail ourselves of our wonderful privilege to pray for others. We long to live the Christ-life of unselfishly yielding our heart unceasingly to God to obtain His blessing for those around us. Intercession then becomes not an incidental or occasional part of our prayers, but their one great object. Our prayer for ourselves takes its true place as the means for preparing us to exercise our ministry of intercession more effectively.

I have humbly asked God to give me what I may give each of my readers—Divine light and help to forsake the life of failure in prayer, and to enter into the life of intercession which the Holy Spirit can enable them to lead. It can be done by a simple act of faith, claiming the fullness of the Spirit, that is, the full measure of the Spirit which you are capable in God's sight of receiving, and He is willing to bestow. Will you not, right now, accept this by faith?

Let me remind you of what takes place when you accept Christ. Most of us sought peace, for a time, in our efforts and struggles to give up sin and please God. But peace was not to be found thus. The peace of God's pardon came by faith, trusting God's promise concerning Christ and His salvation. You had heard of Christ as the gift of God's love; you knew that He was for you, too; you had experienced His grace. But it wasn't until, in faith in God's Word, you accepted Him as God's gift to you, that you found the peace and joy that He can give. Believing in Him and His saving love made all the difference and changed you from someone who had always grieved Him into someone who loved and served

Him. But you still experience times when you feel that you love and serve Him so poorly.

At the time you accepted Christ, you knew little about the Holy Spirit. Later you heard of His dwelling in you, and of His being the power of God in you, making it possible for you to be everything the Father intends you to be. His indwelling and inworking were still vague and indefinite, and hardly a source of joy or strength. You did not yet know how much you might need Him, and, still less, what you might expect of Him. But you have learned from your failures. Now you begin to see how you have been grieving Him by not trusting and not following Him, by not allowing Him to work all God's pleasure in you.

All this can be changed. Just as after seeking Christ—praying to Him, and trying without success to serve Him—you found rest in accepting Him by faith, you can yield yourself to the full guidance of the Holy Spirit in just the same way. Claim and accept Him to work in you whatever God desires. Will you do it? Just accept Him in faith as Christ's gift. Let Him be the Spirit of your whole life (including your prayer life), and you can count on Him to take charge. You can then begin, even though you feel weak and unable to pray properly, to bow before God in silent assurance that He will teach you to pray.

My dear brethren, just as you consciously accepted Christ by faith to pardon your sins, you can now, in the same faith, consciously accept Christ who gives the Holy Spirit to do His work in you. "Christ hath redeemed us...that we might receive the promise of the Spirit by faith" (Galatians 3:13-14). Kneel down, and simply believe that the Lord Jesus Christ, who baptizes with the Holy Spirit, is now, in response to your faith, beginning to bless you with a full experience of the power of the indwelling Spirit. Depend most confidently on Him, regardless of your feelings or your experience, to do His work as the Spirit of supplication and intercession. Renew that act of faith each morning and each time you pray. Trust Him, despite all appearances, to work in you—be sure He is working—and He will show you how the joy of the Holy Spirit can be the power of your life.

"I will pour out the Spirit of supplication." Are you beginning to see that the mystery of prayer is the mystery of the Divine indwelling? God in heaven gives His Spirit to be the Divine power praying in our hearts, drawing us upward to our God. God is a Spirit, and nothing but a similar life and Spirit within us can have communion with Him. Man was created for this communion with God, so that God could dwell and work in him, and be the life of his life. It was this Divine indwelling that sin lost. Christ came to exhibit it in His life, to win it back for us in His death, and then to impart it to us by coming again from heaven in the Spirit to live in His disciples. Only this indwelling of God through the Spirit can explain and enable us to appropriate the wonderful promises given to prayer. God gives the Spirit as a Spirit of supplication, too, to maintain His Divine life within us as a life in which prayer continually rises to heaven.

Without the Holy Spirit, no man can call Jesus Lord, cry, "Abba, Father," worship in spirit and truth, or pray without ceasing. The Holy Spirit is given to the believer to be and do everything in him that God wants him to be and do. He is given to him especially as the Spirit of prayer and supplication. Is it clear that everything in prayer depends on our trusting the Holy Spirit to do His work in us? We must yield ourselves to His leading and depend only and entirely on Him.

We read, "Stephen (was) a man full of faith and of the Holy Spirit" (Acts 6:5). The two always go together in exact proportion to each other. As our faith sees and trusts the Spirit in us to pray, and waits on Him, He will do His work. And our faith— the longing desire and the earnest supplication—our definite faith is all the Father seeks. Do let us know the Holy Spirit, and, in the faith of Christ who unceasingly gives Him, cultivate the assured confidence that we can learn to pray as the Father desires us to pray.

Chapter 11

IN THE NAME OF CHRIST

"Whatsoever ye shall ask in My name, that will I do"—John 14:13.

"If ye shall ask any thing in My name, I will do it"—John 14:14.

"I have chosen you . . . that whatsoever ye shall ask of the Father in My name, He may give it you"—John 15:16.

"Verily, verily, I say unto you, Whatsoever ye shall ask the Father in My name, He will give it you. Hitherto have ye asked nothing in My name: ask, and ye shall receive, that your joy may be full"—John 16:23-24.

"At that day ye shall ask in My name"—John 16:26.

"In My name" is repeated six times. Our Lord knew how slowly our hearts would take this in. He longed so much for us to really believe that His Name is the power in which every knee should bow, and in which every prayer could be heard, that he did not weary of saying it over and over: *"In My name!"*

106

Between the wonderful *whatsoever ye shall ask*, and the Divine *I will do it, the Father will give it,* the simple link is: *"In My name."* Our asking and the Father's giving are equal in the Name of Christ. Everything in prayer depends upon our comprehending this: *"In My name.'*

A name is a word by which we call to mind the whole being and nature of an object. When I speak of a lamb or a lion, the name at once suggests the different nature peculiar to each. The Name of God is meant to express His whole Divine nature and glory. Therefore, the Name of Christ means His whole nature, His person and work, His disposition and Spirit. To ask in the Name of Christ is to pray in union with Him. When a sinner first believes in Christ, he knows and thinks only of His merit and intercession. To the very end, that is the one foundation of our confidence. And yet, as the believer grows in grace and enters more deeply and truly into union with Christ—that is, as he abides in Him—he learns that to pray in the Name of Christ also means to pray in His Spirit. It means to pray in the possession of His nature, as the Holy Spirit imparts it to us. As we grasp the meaning of the words, *"At that day ye shall ask in my name"*—the day when, in the Holy Spirit, Christ came to live in His disciples—we will no longer be staggered at the greatness of the promise: *"Whatsoever* ye shall ask in My name that will I do."* We will get some insight into the unchangeable necessity and certainty of the law that whatever is asked in the Name of Christ, in union with Him and out of His nature and Spirit, must be given.

As Christ's prayer-nature lives in us, His prayer-power becomes ours, too. Our attainment and experience are certainly not the ground of our confidence. Rather, the honesty and whole-heartedness of our surrender to everything that Christ seeks to be in us will determine our spiritual fitness and power to pray in His Name. "If ye abide in me," He says, "ye shall ask what ye will." As we live in Him, we get the spiritual power to avail ourselves of His Name. The branch wholly given up to the life and service of the Vine can count on His sap and strength for its fruit. In the same way, the believer, who, in faith, allows the Spirit to possess his whole life, can avail himself of all the power of Christ's Name.

Here on earth, Christ as man came to reveal what prayer is. To pray in the Name of Christ, we must pray as He prayed on earth—as He taught us to pray—in union with Him—as He now prays in heaven. We must study Him in love and accept Him in faith as our Example, our Teacher, and our Inter-cessor.

Christ Our Example

Prayer in Christ and prayer in us cannot be two different things. Just as there is but one God who is a Spirit and who hears prayer, there is but one spirit of acceptable prayer. We must realize that Christ spent a great deal of time in prayer. The great events of His life were all connected with special prayer. It is important for us to learn of His absolute dependence on, and unceasing direct communication with, the heavenly world if we are able to live a heavenly life, or to exercise heavenly power around us. It is foolish and fruitless to attempt to work for God and heaven without first, in prayer, getting the life and the power of heaven to possess us. Unless this truth lives in us, we cannot avail ourselves of the mighty power of the Name of Christ. His example must teach us the meaning of His Name.

Of His baptism we read, "Jesus also being baptized, *and praying*, the heaven was opened" (Luke 3:21). In prayer, heaven was opened to Him, it came down to Him with the Spirit and the voice of the Father. In power, He was led into the wilderness, in fasting and prayer, this spirit was tested and fully appropriated. Early in His ministry, Mark records (1:35), "And in the morning, . . . a great while before day, He went out, and departed into a solitary place, *and there prayed*." Somewhat later, Luke tells (5:15-16): "Multitudes came together to hear, and to be healed . . . *And He withdrew Himself into the wilderness, and prayed*." He knew how the holy service of preaching and healing could exhaust the spirit. He knew that too much contact with men could cloud the fellowship with God. He knew that time was needed for the Spirit to rest and root in Him, and that no pressure of duty among men could free Him from the absolute need of much prayer. If anyone could have been satisfied with always living and working in the spirit of prayer, it would have been our Master. But He could not. He needed to have His supplies replenished by continual, prolonged seasons of prayer. To use Christ's Name in prayer surely includes following His example and praying as He did.

Of the night before choosing His apostles we read (Luke 6:12): "He went out into a mountain *to pray, and continued all night in prayer to God.*" The first step toward creating the Church and choosing men to be His witnesses and successors called Him to a special prayer of long duration. Everything had to be done according to the pattern established on the mount. "The Son can do nothing of Himself... the Father sheweth Him all things that Himself doeth" (John 5:19-20). In the night of prayer, it was shown to Him.

In the night between the feeding of the five thousand—when Jesus knew that they wanted to take Him by force and make Him King—and the walking on the sea, "He withdrew again into the mountain, Himself alone, to pray" (Matthew 14:23; Mark 6:46; John 6:15). It was God's will He had come to do, and God's power He was to reveal. This power was not a possession of His own; it had to be prayed for and received from above. His first announcement of His approaching death, after He had elicited from Peter the confession that He was the Christ, is introduced by the words (Luke 9:15), "And it came to pass, as *He was alone praying.*" The introduction to the story of the Transfiguration is

(Luke 9:28), He "went up into a mountain *to pray*." The request of the disciples, "Lord, teach us to pray" (Luke 11:1), follows from: "It came to pass, that, *as He was praying* in a certain place." In His own personal life, in His communion with the Father, in everything He is and does for men, the Christ whose Name we are to use is a Man of prayer. Prayer gives Him His power of blessing, and transfigures His very body with the glory of heaven. His own prayer life enables Him to teach others how to pray. How much more must it be prayer—prayer alone, much prayer—that can fit us to share His glory of a trans-figured life, or make us the channel of heavenly blessing and teaching to others? To pray in the Name of Christ is to pray as He prays.

As the end of His life approached, Christ prayed even more. When the Greeks asked to see Him, and He spoke of His approaching death, He prayed. At Lazarus' grave, He prayed. In the last night, He prayed His prayer as our High-Priest, so that we might know what His sacrifice would win, and what His everlasting intercession on the throne would be. In Gethsemane, He prayed His prayer as the Lamb giving itself to the slaughter. Even on the cross, He prayed—a prayer of compassion for His murderers, a prayer of atoning suffering in the thick darkness, a prayer in death of confident resignation of His spirit to the Father.

Christ's life and work, His suffering and death were all prayer. They were all dependence on God, trust in God, receiving from God, surrender to God.

111

Your redemption, O believer, is a redemption brought about by prayer and intercession, because your Christ is a praying Christ. The life He lives for you, the life He lives in you, is a praying life that delights to wait on God and receive everything from Him. To pray in His Name is to pray as He prayed. Christ is our example because He is our Head, our Savior, and our Life. In virtue of His Deity and His Spirit, He can live in us. We can pray in His Name, because we abide in Him and He in us.

Christ Our Teacher

Christ was what He taught. His teaching was the revelation of how He lived, and—praise God—of the life He was to live in us. His teaching of the disciples was to awaken their desire, preparing them for what He would, by the Holy Spirit, be and work in them. Let us believe very confidently that everything He was in prayer, and everything He taught, He himself will give. He came to fulfill the law. But, much more than that, He will fulfill the Gospel in everything taught us about what to pray and how.

What to pray. It has sometimes been said that direct petitions, as compared with the exercise of fellowship with God, are but a subordinate part of prayer, that "in the prayer of those who pray best and most, they occupy an insignificant place." If we carefully study everything that our Lord said about prayer, we see that this is not His teaching. In the Lord's Prayer, in the parables on prayer, in the illustration of a child asking for bread, of our seeking and knocking, in the central thought of the prayer of faith, "Whatsoever ye pray, believe that ye have received," in the often repeated *"whatsoever"* of the last evening—everywhere our Lord urges and encourages us to offer *definite petitions*, and to expect *definite answers*. It is only because we confine prayer too much to our own needs that it is necessary to free it from the appearance of selfishness by giving the petitions a subordinate place. If believers could awaken to the glory of the work of intercession, they would see that in the definite pleading for definite gifts for definite spheres and persons, lies our highest fellowship with our glorified Lord and our only real power to bless men. It would be clear that there can be no truer fellowship with God than these definite petitions and their answers, by which we become the channel of His grace and life to men. It is then that our fellowship with the Father is the same as the Son has in His intercession.

How to pray. Our Lord taught us to pray in secret, in simplicity, with our eyes on God alone, in humility, and in the spirit of forgiving love. But the chief truth He reiterated was this: to pray in faith. And He defined that faith, not only as a trust in God's goodness or power, but as the definite assurance that we have received the very thing we ask for. In the case of a delayed answer, He insisted on perseverance and urgency. We must be followers of those "who through faith and patience inherit the promises" (Hebrews 6:12). This faith accepts the promise and knows it has what it has requested; this patience obtains the promise and inherits the blessing. We then learn to understand why God, who promises to avenge His elect speedily, bears with them in seeming delay. It is so that their faith may be purified from everything that is of the flesh, and tested and strengthened to become that spiritual power that can do all things, even casting mountains into the heart of the sea.

Christ As Our Intercessor

We have gazed on Christ in His prayers; we have listened to His teaching as to how we must pray. To know fully what it is to pray in His Name, we must know Him, too, in His heavenly intercession.

Just think what this means: all His saving work is still carried on in heaven, just as on earth, in unceasing communication with, and direct intercession to, the Father, who is All in All. Every act of grace in Christ has been preceded by, and owes its power to, intercession. God has been honored and acknowledged as its Author. On the throne of God, Christ's highest fellowship with the Father, and His partnership in the Father's rule of the world, is in intercession. Every blessing that comes down to us from above bears this stamp of God: *through Christ's intercession*. His intercession is nothing but the fruit and the glory of His atonement. When He gave Himself as a sacrifice to God for men, He proved that His whole heart had the one object of glorifying God in the salvation of men. In His intercession, this great purpose is realized: He glorifies the Father by asking and receiving everything from Him. He saves men by bestowing on them what He has obtained from the Father. Christ's intercession is the Father's glory, His own glory, and our glory.

And now this Christ, the Intercessor, is our life. He is our Head and we are His body. His Spirit and life breathe in us. On earth, as in heaven, intercession is God's chosen, God's only, channel of blessing. Let us learn from Christ what glory there is in it, what the way to exercise this wondrous power is, and what part it is to take in our work for God.

The glory of it. By it, beyond anything, we glorify God. By it we glorify Christ. By it we bring blessing to the Church and the world. By it we obtain our highest nobility—the Godlike power of saving men.

The way to it. Paul writes, "Walk in love, as Christ also hath loved us, and gave Himself...a sacrifice to God for us" (Ephesians 5:2). If we live as Christ lives, we will give ourselves—our whole life— to God, to be used by Him for men. When we have done this, we will no longer seek anything for ourselves, but for men. And, when we ask God to use us, and to impart to us what we can bestow on others, intercession will become to us, as it is in Christ in heaven, the great work of our life. And, if we ever think that the call is too high, or the work too great, faith in the Interceding Christ, who lives in us, will give us the victory. We will listen to Him who said, "The works that I do shall he do also; and greater works than these shall he do" (John 14:12). We will remember that we are not under the law, with its impotence, but under grace with its omnipotence, working all in us. We will believe again in Him who said to us, "Rise and walk," and gave us His life as our strength. We will claim afresh the fullness of God's Spirit as His sufficient provision for our needs, and rely on Him to be in us the Spirit of Intercession, who makes us one with Christ. O! let us only keep our place—giving up ourselves, like Him, in Him, to God for men.

Then, we will understand the role intercession is to have in God's work through us. We will no longer try to work for God, and ask Him to follow it with His blessing. We will do what the friend at midnight did, what Christ did on earth, and forever does in heaven—we will first get from God, and then turn to men to give what He gave us. As with Christ, we will make our chief work to receive from the Father. Giving to men will then be in power.

Servants of Christ! children of God! be of good courage. Let no fear of weakness or poverty make you afraid—ask in the Name of Christ. His Name is Himself, in all His perfection and power. He is the living Christ, and will Himself make His Name a power in you. Do not fear to plead the Name. His promise is a threefold cord that cannot be broken. *Whatsoever ye ask—in My Name—it shall be done unto you.*

Chapter 12

MY GOD WILL HEAR ME

"Therefore will the Lord wait, that He may be gracious unto you . . . . Blessed are all they that wait for Him . . . . He will be very gracious unto thee at the voice of thy cry; when He shall hear it, He will answer thee"—Isaiah 30:18-19.

"The Lord will hear when I call unto Him"—Psalm 4:3.

"I have called upon Thee, for Thou wilt hear me, O God"—Psalm 17:6.

"I will look unto the Lord; I will wait for the God of my salvation: my God will hear me"—Micah 7:7.

The power of prayer rests in the faith that God hearts it. In more than one sense, this is true. It is this faith that gives a man courage to pray. It is this faith that gives him power to prevail with God. The moment I am assured that God hears *me*, too, I feel drawn to pray and to persevere in prayer. I feel the strength to claim and take in faith the answer God gives. The main reason for the lack of prayer is the want of the living, joyous assurance: "My God will hear me." If only God's servants had a vision of the living God waiting to grant their request—to bestow all the heavenly gifts of the Spirit they are in need of—how everything would be set aside to make room for this one power that can ensure heavenly blessing—the prayer of faith!

When a man can and does say, in living faith, "My God will hear me!" nothing can keep him from prayer. He knows that what he cannot do or get done on earth, can and will be done for him from heaven. Let each one of us bow in stillness before God, and wait on Him to reveal Himself to us as the prayer-bearing God. In His presence, the wondrous thoughts gathering round the central truth will be revealed to us.

1. *"My God will hear me." What a blessed certainty!* We have God's word for it in numberless promises. We have thousands of witnesses who will attest to the fact that they have found it to be true. We have had the experience of it in our lives. We have known it to be true. We have had the Son of God come from heaven with the message that, if we ask, the Father will give. We have had Christ Himself praying on earth, and being heard. And we have Him in heaven now, sitting at the right hand of God and making intercession for us. God hears prayer— *God delights to hear prayer*. He has allowed His people to be tried a thousand times over, that they might be compelled to cry to Him, and learn to know Him as the Hearer of prayer.

Let us confess with shame how little we have believed this wondrous truth. How seldom we have received it into our heart, and allowed it to possess and control our whole being. That we accept a truth is not enough. The living God, of whom the truth speaks, must, in its light, be so revealed that our whole life is spent in His presence. Our consciousness must be as clear as a little child's toward its earthly parent—I know for certain my father hears me.

Beloved child of God! you know by experience how little an intellectual understanding of truth has profited you. Beseech God to reveal Himself to you. If you want to live a different prayer life, bow each time before you pray in silence to worship God. Wait there until some right sense of His nearness and readiness to answer comes to you. You will begin to pray with the words, "My God will hear me!"

2. *"My God will hear me." What a wondrous grace!* Think of God in His infinite majesty, His altogether incomprehensible glory, His unapproachable holiness, sitting on a throne of grace, waiting to be gracious, inviting, and encouraging you to pray with His promise: "Call upon Me, and I will answer thee" (Psalm 91:15). Think of yourself— your nothingness and helplessness as a man, your wretchedness and transgressions as a sinner, your feebleness and unworthiness as a saint—and praise the glory of that grace which allows you to say boldly of your prayer for yourself and others, "My God will hear me." Think of how you are not left to

yourself, and of what you can accomplish in this wonderful fellowship with God. God has united you with Christ; in Him and His Name, you have your confidence. On the throne, He prays *with* you and *for* you; on the footstool of the throne, you pray *with* Him and *in* Him. His worth, and the Father's delight in hearing ˙Him, are the measure of your confidence—your assurance of being heard.

There is more. Think of the Holy Spirit, the Spirit of God's own Son, sent into your heart to cry, Abba, Father. The Holy Spirit is to be *in you* a Spirit of supplication, when you do not know how to pray as you ought. Think, in all your insignificance and unworthiness, of your being as acceptable as Christ Himself. Think, in all your ignorance and feebleness, of the Spirit making intercession according to God within you. Then, cry out, "What wondrous grace! Through Christ I have access to the Father, by the Spirit. I can, I do believe it: 'My God will hear me.' "

3. *"My God will hear me." What a deep mystery!* Sometimes, difficulties arise that cannot help but perplex even the honest heart. There is the question as to God's sovereign, all-wise, all-disposing will. How can our wishes, often so foolish, and our will, often so selfish, overrule or change that perfect will? Is it not better to leave all to His disposal, who knows what is best, and loves to give us the very best? Or, how can our prayer change what He has ordained before? Then, there is the question as to the need of persevering prayer, and waiting long for the

answer. If God is infinite love and delights more to give than we to receive, what is the need for the pleading, wrestling, urgency, and long delay of which Scripture and experience speak? Arising out of this, there is still another question—that of the multitude of apparently vain and unanswered prayers. How many have pleaded for loved ones, and they appeared to die unsaved. How many cry for years for spiritual blessing, and no answer comes. To think of all this tries our faith, and makes us hesitate as we say, "My God will hear me."

Beloved! prayer, in its power with God, and His faithfulness to His promise to hear it, is a deep, spiritual mystery. To the above questions, answers can be given which remove some of the difficulty. But, after all, the first and the last that must be said is this: As little as we can comprehend God can we comprehend this, one of the most blessed of His attributes, that He hears prayer. It is a spiritual mystery—nothing less than the mystery of the Holy Trinity. God hears because we pray in His Son, because the Holy Spirit prays in us.

If we have believed and claimed the life of Christ as our health, and the fullness of the Spirit as our strength, let us not hesitate to believe in the power of our prayer, too. The Holy Spirit can enable us to believe and rejoice in it, even where every question is not yet answered. He will do this as we lay our questionings in God's bosom, trust His faithfulness, and give ourselves humbly to obey His command to pray without ceasing. Every art unfolds its secrets and its beauty only to the man who practices it. To the humble soul who prays in the obedience of faith, who practices prayer and intercession diligently because God asks it, the secret of the Lord will be revealed. To this soul, the thought of the deep mystery of prayer, instead of being a weary problem, will be a source of rejoicing, adoration, and faith, in which the unceasing refrain is ever heard: *"My God will hear me!"*

4. *"My God will hear me." What a solemn responsibility!* How often we complain about darkness, feebleness, and failure, as if there were no help for them. God has promised, in answer to our prayer, to supply our every need, and give us His light and strength and peace. If we only realized the responsibility of having such a God, and such promises, with the sin and shame of not fully availing ourselves of them. How confident we should feel that the grace, which we have accepted and trusted to enable us to pray as we should, will be given.

There is more. This access to a prayer-hearing God is especially meant to make us intercessors for our fellow-men. Even as Christ obtained His right of prevailing intercession by giving Himself as a sacrifice to God for men, and through it receives the blessings He dispenses, so, if we have truly given ourselves to God, we share His right of intercession, and are able to obtain the powers of the heavenly world, too. The power of life and death is in our hand (1 John 5:16). In answer to prayer, the Spirit can be poured out; souls can be converted; believers can be established. In prayer, the kingdom of darkness can be conquered, souls brought out of prison into the liberty of Christ, and the glory of God be revealed. Through prayer, the sword of the Spirit—the Word of God—can be wielded in power, and, in public preaching as in private speaking, the most rebellious made to bow at Jesus' feet.

What a responsibility the Church has in giving herself to the work of intercession! What a responsibility every minister, missionary, worker, set apart for the saving of souls, has in yielding himself wholly to act out and prove his faith: "My God will hear me!" And what a call on every believer, instead of burying and losing this talent, to seek to use it to the very utmost in prayer and supplication for all saints and for all men. My God will hear me. The deeper our entrance into the truth of this wondrous power God has given to men, the more wholehearted our surrender to the work of intercession will be.

5. *"My God will hear me."* What a blessed *prospect!* I see that all the failures of my past life have been due to the lack of this faith. My failure, especially in the work of intercession, has had its deepest root in this—I did not live in the full faith of the blessed assurance, *"My God will hear me!"* Praise God! I begin to see it—I believe it. All can be different. Or, rather, I see Him; I believe Him. *"My God will hear me!"* Yes, me, even me! Commonplace and insignificant though I be, filling but a very little place, so that I will hardly be missed when I go—even *I* have access to this Infinite God, with the

123

confidence that He hears me. One with Christ, led by the Holy Spirit, I dare to say, "I will pray for others, for I am sure my God will listen to me: *'My God will hear me!'* " What a blessed prospect before me—every earthly and spiritual anxiety is exchanged for the peace of God, who cares for all and hears prayer. What a blessed prospect in my work—to know that even when the answer is long in coming, and there is a call for much patient, persevering prayer, the truth remains infallibly sure—*"My God will hear me!"*

And what a blessed prospect for Christ's Church if we could all give prayer its place, give faith in God its place or, rather, *give the prayer-hearing God His place!* This is the one great thing which those who, in some measure, begin to see the urgent need of prayer should pray for in the first place. When God, at first, and then time after time, poured forth the Spirit on His praying people, He laid down the law for all time: as much of prayer, so much of the Spirit. Let each one who can say, *"My God will hear me,"* join in the fervent supplication that, throughout the Church, truth may be restored to its true place, and the blessed prospect will be realized: a praying Church overflowing with the power of the Holy Spirit.

6. *"My God will hear me." What a need of Divine teaching!* We need this, both to enable us to hold this word in living faith, and to make full use of it in intercession. It has been said, and it cannot be said too often or too earnestly, that the one necessary thing for the Church of our day is the power of

the Holy Spirit. It is just because this is so, from the Divine side, that we may also say that, from the human side, the one necessary thing is more prayer—more believing, persevering prayer. There is much to be confessed and taken away in us if the Spirit is to work freely. But, the upward look, the deep dependence, the strong crying to God, and the effectual prayer of faith that avails—all these are sadly lacking. And all these are essential.

Shouldn't we all try to learn the lesson which will make prevailing prayer possible—the lesson of a faith that always sings, *"My God will hear me"*? Simple and elementary as it is, it requires practice, patience, time, and heavenly teaching to learn it correctly. Under the impression of a bright thought or a blessed experience, it may look as if we knew the lesson perfectly. But the need of making this our first prayer—that God who hears prayer would teach us to believe it, and so to pray correctly—will continually recur. If we desire it, we can count on Him. He delights in hearing prayer and answering it. He gave His Son that He might always pray *for* us and *with* us, and His Holy Spirit to pray *in* us. We can be sure there is not a prayer that He will hear more certainly than this: that He so reveal Himself as the prayer-hearing God, that our whole being may respond, *"My God will hear me."*

Chapter 13

PAUL: A PATTERN OF PRAYER

"Go . . . and inquire . . . for one called Saul, of Tarsus: for, behold, he prayeth"—Acts 9:11.

"For this cause I obtained mercy, that in me first Jesus Christ might shew forth all longsuffering, for a pattern to them which should hereafter believe on Him to life everlasting"—1 Timothy 1:16.

God took His own Son and made Him our example and our pattern. It sometimes is as if the power of Christ's example is lost in the thought that He, in whom is no sin, is not man as we are. Our Lord took Paul, a man of like passions with ourselves, and made him a pattern of what He could do for one who was the chief of sinners. And Paul, the man who, more than any other, has set his mark on the Church, has always been thought of as an exemplary man. In his mastery of Divine truth, and his teaching of it; in his devotion to his Lord, and his self-consuming zeal in His service; in his deep experience of the power of the indwelling Christ and the fellowship of His cross; in the sincerity of his humility, and the simplicity and boldness of his faith; in his missionary enthusiasm and endurance—in all this, and so much more, "the grace of our Lord was exceeding abundant" (1 Timothy 1:14). Christ gave him, and the Church has accepted him, as a pattern of what Christ would have, of what Christ would work. Seven times Paul speaks of believers following him: "Wherefore I beseech you, be ye followers of me" (1 Corinthians 4:16); "Be ye followers of me, even as I am of Christ" (1 Corinthians 11:1); (and also in Philippians 3:17; 4:9; 1 Thessalonians 1:6; 2 Thessalonians 3:7-9).

If Paul, as a pattern of prayer, is not studied or appealed to as much as he is in other respects, it is not because he is not a remarkable proof of what grace can do, or because we do not, in this respect, stand in as much need of the help of his example. A study of Paul as a pattern of prayer will bring a rich reward of instructions, and encouragment. The words our Lord used of Paul at his conversion, "Behold he prayeth" (Acts 9:11), may be taken as the keynote of his life from then on. Christ at the right hand of God, in whom we are blessed with all spiritual blessings, was everything to him. To pray and expect the heavenly power *in* his work and *on* his work, coming directly from heaven by prayer, was the simple outcome of his faith in the Glorified One. In this, too, Christ meant him to be a pattern, so that we might learn that just as Christ and His gifts, and the unworldliness of the powers that work for salvation are known and believed, prayer will become the spontaneous rising of the heart to the only source of its life. Let us see what we know of Paul.

Paul's Habits of Prayer

These habits are revealed almost unconsciously. He writes in Romans 1:9, 11: "God is my witness...that without ceasing I make mention of you *always in my prayers*...For I long to see you, that I may impart unto you some spiritual gift, to the end ye may be established." In Romans 10:1; 9:2-3: "My *heart's desire and prayer to God* for Israel is, that they may be saved"; "I have great heaviness and *continual sorrow of heart*. For I could wish that myself were accursed from Christ for my brethren." In 1 Corinthians 1:4: "I thank my God *always* on your behalf, for the grace of God which is given you by Jesus Christ." In 2 Corinthians 6:4-5: "Approving ourselves as the ministers of God...*in watchings, in fastings*." In Galatians 4:19: "My little children, of whom *I travail in birth again until* Christ be formed in you." In Ephesians 1:16: "*I cease not* to give thanks for you, making mention of you *in my prayers*." In Ephesians 3:14: "*I bow my knees* unto the Father...that He would grant you...to be strengthened with might by His Spirit in the inner man." In Philippians 1:3-4,8-9: "I thank my God *upon every remembrance of you, always in every prayer of mine* for you all making request with joy....For God is my record, how greatly I long after you all in the bowels of Jesus Christ. And this *I pray.*" In Colossians 1:3,9: "We give thanks to God ...*praying always for you.* For this cause we also, since the day we heard it, *do not cease to pray for you*, and to desire." In Colossians 2:1: "I would that ye knew what *great conflict* I have for you....and for as many as have not seen my face in the flesh." In 1 Thessalonians 1:2: "We give thanks to God *always* for you all, making mention of you *in our prayers.*" In 1 Thessalonians 3:9-10: "We joy for your sakes before our God; *night and day praying exceedingly* that we...might perfect that which is lacking in your faith." In 1 Thessalonians 1:3,11: "We are bound to thank God *always* for you....Wherefore also *we always pray* for you." In 2 Timothy 1:3: "I thank God...that *without ceasing* I have remembrance of thee...night and day." In Philemon 4: "I thank my God, making mention of thee *always in my prayers.*"

These passages taken together give us the picture of a man whose words, "Pray without ceasing," were simply the expression of his daily life. He had such a sense of the insufficiency of simple conversion; of the need of the grace and the power of heaven being brought down for the young converts in prayer; of the need of much and unceasing prayer, day and night, to bring it down; of the certainty that prayer would bring it down—that his life was continual and most definite prayer. He had such a sense that everything must come from above, and such a faith that it would come in answer to prayer, that prayer was neither a duty nor a burden, but the natural turning of the heart to the only place whence it could possibly obtain what it sought for others.

The Contents of Paul's Prayers

It is of as much importance to know *what* Paul prayed, as how frequently and earnestly he did so. Intercession is a spiritual work. Our confidence in it will greatly depend on our knowing that we ask according to the will of God. The more distinctly we ask heavenly things—which we feel God alone can bestow, which we are sure He *will* bestow—the more direct and urgent our appeal to God alone will be. The more impossible the things are that we seek, the more we will turn from all human work to prayer and to God alone.

In the Epistles, in addition to where he speaks of his praying, we have a number of distinct prayers in which Paul utters his heart's desire for those to whom he writes. In these we see that his first desire was always that they might be "established" in the Christian life. As much as he praised God when he heard of conversion, he knew how feeble the young converts were—how their establishing would avail nothing without the grace of the Spirit prayed down. If we look at some of his major prayers, we will see what he asked and obtained.

Take the two prayers in Ephesians—the one for light, the other for strength. In the former (1:15), he prays for the Spirit of wisdom to enlighten them to know what their calling and inheritance was. It was also so they would know about the mighty power of God working in them. Spiritual enlightenment and knowledge was their great need, to be obtained for them by prayer. In the latter (3:15), he asks that the power they had been led to see in Christ might work in them. He asks that they be strengthened with Divine might, so as to have the indwelling Christ, the love that passes knowledge, and the fullness of God actually come on them. These were things that could only come directly from heaven. These were things he asked and expected. If we want to learn Paul's art of intercession, we must ask nothing less for believers in our days.

Look at the prayer in Philippians (1:9-11). There, too, it is first for spiritual knowledge; then comes a blameless life, and then a fruitful life to the glory of God. It is also so in the beautiful prayer in Colossians (1:9-11). First, spiritual knowledge and understanding of God's will, then the strengthening with all might to all patience and joy.

Or, take the two prayers in 1 Thessalonians (3:12-13;5:23). The one: "The Lord make you to increase and abound in love one toward another...To the end that He may stablish your hearts unblameable in holiness." The other: "May the God of peace sanctify you wholly; and I pray God your whole spirit and soul and body be preserved blameless." The very words are so high that we hardly understand, still less believe, still less experience what they mean. Paul so lived in the heavenly world—he was so at home in the holiness and omnipotence of God and His love—that such prayers were the natural expression of what he knew God could and would do. "God stablish your hearts unblameable in holiness"; "God sanctify you wholly"—the man who believes in these things and desires them will pray for them for others. The prayers are all a proof that Paul seeks for them the very life of heaven on earth. No wonder that he is not tempted to trust in any human means, but looks for it from heaven alone. Again, I say, the more we take Paul's prayers as our pattern, and make his desires our own for believers for whom we pray, the more prayer to the God of heaven will become as our daily breath.

Paul's Requests for Prayer

These are no less instructive than his own prayers for the saints. They prove that he does not consider prayer any special prerogative of an apostle. He calls the humblest and simplest believer to claim his right. They prove that he does not think that only the new converts or feeble Christians need prayer. He himself is, as a member of the body, dependent on his brethren and their prayers. After he had preached the gospel for twenty years, he still asked for prayer that he might speak as he ought to. Not once and for all, not for a time, but day by day, without ceasing, must grace be sought and brought down from heaven for his work. United, continued waiting on God is to Paul the only hope of the Church. With the Holy Spirit, a heavenly life—the life of the Lord in heaven—entered the world. Nothing but unbroken communication with heaven can keep it up.

Listen to how he asks for prayer, and with what earnestness—"*I beseech you*, brethren, for the Lord Jesus Christ's sake, and for the love of the Spirit, that *ye strive together with me in your prayers* to God for me; that I may be delivered from them which do not believe in Judea...and may come unto you with joy by the will of God" (Romans 15:30-32). How remarkably both prayers were answered: Romans 15:5-6,13. The remarkable fact that the Roman world-power had proved its antagonism to God's Kingdom, then all at once becomes Paul's protector, and secures him a safe convoy to Rome, can only be accounted for by these prayers.

In 2 Corinthians 1:10-11: "In whom we trust that He will yet deliver us; *ye also helping together by prayer* for us." In Ephesians 6:18-20: "Praying always with all prayer and supplication in the Spirit ...for all saints; *and for me*...that I may open my mouth boldly...that therein I may speak boldly, as I ought to speak." In Philippians 1:19: "I know that this (trouble) shall turn to my salvation *through your prayer*, and the supply of the Spirit of Jesus Christ." In Colossians 4:2-4: "Continue in prayer ...withal *praying also for us*, that God would open unto us a door of utterance, to speak the mystery of Christ...that I may make it manifest, as I ought to speak." In 1 Thessalonians 5:25: "Brethren, pray for us." In Philemon 22: "I trust that through your prayers I shall be given to you."

We saw how Christ prayed, and taught His disciples to pray. We see how Paul prayed, and taught the churches to pray. As the Master, so the servant calls us to believe and to prove that prayer is the power both of the ministry and the Church. We have a summary of his faith in these remarkable words concerning something which caused him grief: "This shall turn to my salvation through your prayer, and the supply of the Spirit of Jesus Christ." As much as he looked to his Lord in heaven, he looked to his brethren on earth to secure the supply of that Spirit for him. The Spirit from heaven and prayer on earth were to him, as to the twelve after Pentecost, inseparably linked. We often speak of apostolic zeal and devotion and power—may God give us a revival of apostolic prayer.

Let me ask once again, does the work of intercession take the place in the Church it ought to have? Is it commonly understood that everything depends on getting from God that "supply of the Spirit of Christ" for and in ourselves which can give our work its real power to bless? This is Christ's Divine order for all work—His own and that of His servants. This is the order Paul followed: first come every day, as having nothing, and receive from God "the supply of the Spirit" in intercession; then go and impart what has come to you from heaven.

In all His instructions, our Lord Jesus spoke

more often to His disciples about their praying than their preaching. In the farewell discourse, He said little about preaching, but much about the Holy Spirit, and their asking "whatsoever they would in His name." If we are to return to this life of the first apostles and of Paul, and really accept the truth that our only strength is intercession, we must have the courage to confess past sins and to believe that there is deliverance. To break through old habits, to resist the clamor of pressing duties that have always had their way, to make every other call subordinate to this one, whether others approve or not, will not be easy at first. But the men or women who are faithful will not only be rewarded themselves, but they will become benefactors to their brethren. "Thou shalt be called, the repairer of the breach, the restorer of paths to dwell in" (Isaiah 58:12).

But is it really possible? Can it indeed be that those who have never been able to face, much less overcome, the difficulty can become mighty in prayer? Tell me, was it really possible for Jacob to become Israel—a prince who prevailed with God? It was. The things that are impossible with men are possible with God. Have you not received from the Father, as the great fruit of Christ's redemption, the Spirit of supplication, the Spirit of intercession? Just pause and think what that means. And will you still doubt whether God is able to make you "strivers with God," princes who prevail with Him? Oh, let us abandon all fear, and in faith claim the grace for which we have the Holy Spirit dwelling in us—the grace of supplication, the grace of intercession. Let us quietly, perseveringly believe that He lives in us and will enable us to do our work. Let us in faith not fear to accept and yield to the great truth that intercession, as it is the great work of the King on the throne, *is the great work of His servants on earth.* We have the Holy Spirit, who brings the Christ-life into our hearts, to fit us for this work. Let us at once realize and arouse the gift within us. As we daily set aside our time for intercession, and count on the Spirit's enabling power, the confidence that we can, in our measure, follow even as he followed Christ will grow.

Chapter 14

GOD SEEKS INTERCESSORS

"I have set watchmen upon thy walls, O Jerusalem, which shall never hold their peace day nor night: ye that make mention of the Lord, keep not silence, and give Him no rest ... till He makes Jerusalem a praise in the earth"—Isaiah 62:6-7.

"And He saw that there was no man, and wondered that there was no intercessor"—Isaiah 59:16.

"And I looked, and there was none to help; and I wondered that there was none to uphold"—Isaiah 63:5.

"There is none that calleth upon Thy name, that stirreth up himself to take hold of Thee"—Isaiah 64:7.

"And I sought for a man ... that should ... stand in the gap before Me for the land, that I should not destroy it: but I found none"—Ezekiel 22:30.

"I have chosen you, and ordained you, that ye should go and bring forth fruit ... that whatsoever ye shall ask of the Father in My name, He may give it you"—John 15:16.

In the study of the starry heavens, much depends on proper understanding of magnitudes. Without some sense of the size of the heavenly bodies, which appear so small to the eye, and of the almost unlimited extent of the regions in which they move, though they appear so near, there can be no true knowledge of the heavenly world or its relation to this earth. It is even so with the spiritual heavens and the heavenly life in which we are called to live. It is especially so in the life of intercession, that most wondrous fellowship between heaven and earth. Everything depends on the proper understanding of magnitudes.

Just think of the three that come first. There is a world, with its needs entirely dependent on and waiting to be helped by intercession. There is a God in heaven, with His all-sufficient supply for all those needs, waiting to be asked. There is a Church, with its wondrous calling and its sure promises, waiting to be roused to a sense of its wondrous responsibility and power.

God seeks intercessors. There is a world with its perishing millions, with intercession as its only hope. So much love and work are comparatively vain, because there is so little intercession. There are millions living as if there had never been a Son of God to die for them. Every year, millions pass into the outer darkness without hope. Millions bear the Christian name, but the great majority of them live in utter ignorance or indifference. Millions of feeble, sickly Christians, thousands of wearied workers, could be blessed by intercession, could help themselves to become mighty in intercession. Churches and missions sacrificing life and labor with little result often lack the power of intercession. Souls, each one worth more than worlds—worth nothing less than the price paid for them in Christ's blood—are within reach of the power that can be won by intercession. We surely have no conception of the magnitude of the work to be done by God's intercessors, or we would cry to God above everything to give us the spirit of intercession.

God seeks intercessors. There is a God of glory able to meet all these needs. We are told that He delights in mercy, that He waits to be gracious, that He longs to pour out His blessing. We are told that the love which gave the Son up to death is the same love that each moment hovers over every human being. And yet He does not help. And there they perish. It is as if God does not move. If He does so love and long to bless, there must be some inscrutable reason for His holding back. What can it be? Scripture says it is because of your unbelief. It is the faithlessness and consequent unfaithfulness of God's people. He has taken them up into partnership with Himself. He has honored them, and bound Himself, by making their prayers one of the standard measures of the working of His power. Lack of intercession is one of the chief reasons for the lack of blessing. O that we would turn our eyes and heart from everything else and fix them on this God who hears prayer. Let the magnificence of His promises,

His power, and His purpose of love overwhelm us! How our whole life and heart would become intercession.

God seeks intercessors. There is a third magnitude to which our eyes must be opened: the wondrous privilege and power of the intercessors. There is a false humility which makes a great virtue of self-depreciation, because it has never seen its utter nothingness. If it knew that, it would never apologize for its feebleness, but glory in its utter weakness as the one condition of Christ's power resting on it. It would judge itself, its power, and influence before God in prayer as little by what it sees or feels as we judge the size of the sun or stars by what the eye can see. Faith sees man created in God's image and likeness to be God's representative in this world and have dominion over it. Faith sees man redeemed and lifted into union with Christ—abiding in Him, identified with Him, and clothed with His power in intercession. Faith sees the Holy Spirit dwelling and praying in the heart, making, in our sighings, intercession to God. Faith sees the intercession of the saints as part of the life of the Holy Trinity—the believer as God's child asking of the Father, in the Son, through the Spirit. Faith sees something of the Divine fitness and beauty of this scheme of salvation through intercession. Faith wakens the soul to a consciousness of its wondrous destiny, and arms it with strength for the blessed self-sacrifice it calls to.

God seeks intercessors. When He called His people out of Egypt, He separated the priestly tribe to draw near to Him, stand before Him, and bless the people in His name. From time to time, He sought and found and honored intercessors, for whose sake He spared or blessed His people. When our Lord left the earth, He said to the inner circle He had gathered around Him—an inner circle of special devotion to His service, to which access is still free to every disciple: "I have chosen you, and ordained you, that whatsoever ye shall ask of the Father in My name, He may give it you." We have already noticed the three wonderful words repeated six times— *Whatsoever*—In My Name—*It shall be done.* In them, Christ placed the power of the heavenly world at their disposal—not for their own selfish use, but in the interest of His Kingdom. We know how wondrously they used it. And since that time, down through the ages, these men have had their successors, men who have proved how surely God works in answer to prayer. And we may praise God that in our days, too, there is an ever-increasing number who begin to see and prove that in church and mission, in all societies, large and small, intercession is the chief thing. They see that it is the power that moves God and opens heaven. They are learning and long to learn better so that all may learn—that in our work for souls, intercession must take the first place. Those who have received from heaven, in the power of the Holy Spirit, what they are to communicate to others will be best able to do the Lord's work.

God seeks intercessors. Though God had His appointed servants in Israel—watchmen set by Himself to cry to Him day and night and give Him no rest—He often had to wonder and complain that there was no intercessor. He wondered why there was no one who stirred himself up to take hold of His strength. And He still waits and wonders in our day that there are not more intercessors. He still wonders why all of His children do not give themselves to this highest and holiest work, and why many of them who do so, do not engage in it more intensely and perseveringly. He wonders why ministers of His gospel complain that their duties do not allow them to find time for this, which He considers their first, highest, most delightful, and alone effective work. He wonders why His sons and daughters, who have forsaken home and friends for His sake, come so short in what He meant to be their abiding strength—receiving day by day all they need to impart to the non-believers. He wonders why multitudes of His children have little conception of what intercession is. He wonders why even more have learned that it is their duty, seek to obey it, but confess that they know little about taking hold of God or prevailing with Him.

God seeks intercessors. He longs to dispense larger blessings. He longs to reveal His power and glory as God, His saving love, more abundantly. He seeks intercessors in larger number, in greater power, to prepare the way of the Lord. He seeks them. Where could He seek them but in His Church? And how does He expect to find them? He entrusted to His Church the task of telling about their Lord's need, of encouraging, training, and preparing them for His holy service. And He always comes again, seeking fruit, seeking intercessors. In His Word, He has spoken of the "widow indeed, (who) trusteth in God, and continueth in supplications and prayers night and day" (1 Timothy 5:5).

God seeks intercessors. He looks to see if the Church is training the great army of aged men and women, whose time of outward work is past, but who can strengthen the army of the "elect, which cry day and night unto Him" (Luke 18:7). He looks to the great host of the Christian endeavor—the three or four million young lives given in the solemn pledge: I promise the Lord Jesus Christ that I will strive to do whatever He would like to have me do—and wonders how many are being trained to pass from the brightness of the weekly prayer-meeting and its confession of loyalty, on to the secret intercession that is to save souls. He looks to the thousands of young men and women in training for the work of ministry and mission. He gazes long-ingly to see if the Church is teaching them that intercession—power with God—must be their first care. The Church should seek to train and help them to do it. He looks to see whether ministers and missionaries are understanding their opportunity, and laboring to turn the believers of their congregation into those who can "help together" by their prayer, and can "strive with them in their prayers." As Christ seeks the lost sheep until He finds it, God seeks intercessors.

God seeks intercessors. He will not, He cannot, take the work out of the hands of His Church. And so He comes, calling and pleading in many ways. Now, by a man whom He raises up to live a life of faith in His service, and to prove how actually and abundantly He answers prayer. Then, by the story of a church which makes prayer for souls its starting point, and bears testimony to God's faithfulness. Sometimes, in a mission which proves how special prayer can meet special need, and bring down the power of the Spirit. Or other times, by a season of revival coming in answer to united, urgent supplication. In these and many other ways, God is showing us what intercession can do. He is beseeching us to awaken and train His great host to be, every one, a people of intercession.

God seeks intercessors. He sends His servants out to call them. Let ministers make this a part of their duty. Let them make their church a training school of intercession. Give the people definite objects for prayer. Encourage them to make a definite time for it, even if it is only ten minutes every day. Help them to understand the boldness they may use with God. Teach them to expect and look for answers. Show them what it is first to pray and get an answer in secret, and then carry the answer and impart the blessing. Tell everyone who is master of his own time that he is as the angels—free to tarry before the throne and then go out and minister to the heirs of salvation. Sound out the blessed tidings that this honor is for all God's people. There is no difference. That servant girl, this day laborer, that bedridden invalid, this daughter in her mother's home, these men in business—all are called, *all, all,* are needed. God seeks intercessors.

God seeks intercessors. As ministers begin the work of finding and training intercessors, it will urge them to pray more themselves. Christ made Paul a pattern of His grace before He made him a preacher of it. It has been well said, "The first duty of a clergyman is humbly to beg of God that all he would have done in his people may be first truly and fully done in himself." The effort to bring this message of God may cause much heart-searching and humiliation. All the better. The best practice in doing a thing is helping others to do it. O servants of Christ, be as watchmen who cry to God day and night. Let us awake to our holy calling. Let us believe in the power of intercession. Let us practice it. Let us seek on behalf of our people to get from God Himself the Spirit and the life we preach. With our spirit and life given up to God in intercession, the Spirit and life that God gives them through us cannot fail to be the life of intercession, too.

Chapter 15

THE COMING REVIVAL

"Wilt Thou not revive us again: that Thy people may rejoice in Thee?"—Psalm 85:6.

"O Lord, revive Thy work in the midst of the years"—Habakkuk 3:2.

"Though I walk in the midst of trouble, Thou wilt revive me . . . Thy right hand shall save me"—Psalm 138:7.

"I dwell . . . with Him also that is of a contrite and humble spirit . . . to revive the heart of the contrite ones"—Isaiah 57:15.

"Come and let us return unto the Lord: for He hath torn, and He will heal us . . . He will revive us"—Hosea 6:1-2.

The coming revival—one frequently hears these words. There are many teachers who see signs of its approach, and confidently herald its speedy appearance. In the increase of mission interest, in the tidings of revivals in heathen places where Christian doors are opening, in the hosts of our young, in victories already secured—wherever believing, hopeful workers enter—they are given the assurance of a time of power and blessing such as we have never known. They are told that the Church is about to enter into a new era of increasing spirituality and larger extension.

There are others who, while admitting the truth of some of these facts, fear that the conclusion drawn from them are one-sided and premature. They see the interest in missions increased, but point out to how small a circle it is confined. They also note how utterly out of proportion it is to what it ought to be. To the great majority of Church members—to the greater part of the Church—it is as yet anything but a life question. They remind us of the power of worldliness and formality. They contrast the increase of the money-making and pleasure-loving spirit among professing Christians, to the lack of spirituality in so many, many of our churches. They declare that the continuing and apparently increasing estrangement of many from God's Day and Word is proof that the great revival has certainly not begun, and is hardly thought of by most. They say that they do not see the deep humiliation, the intense desire, and the fervent prayer which appear as forerunners of every true revival.

These are two opposing views which are equally dangerous. We must guard against both superficial optimism, which is never able to gauge the extent of the evil, and hopeless pessimism, which neither praises God for what He has done, nor trusts Him for what He is ready to do.

Optimism will lose itself in happy self-congratulation, as it rejoices in its zeal and diligence and apparent success. It will never see the need of confession and great striving in prayer so we can be prepared to meet and conquer the hosts of darkness. Pessimism virtually gives over the world to Satan, and almost prays and rejoices to see things get worse. It will hasten the coming of Him who is to make all right. May God keep us from either error, and fulfill the promise, "Thine ears shall hear a word behind thee, saying, This is the way, walk ye in it, when ye turn to the right hand, and when ye turn to the left" (Isaiah 30:21).

Let us listen to the lessons suggested by the passages we have quoted. They may help us to pray the prayer correctly "Revive Thy work, O Lord!"

1. *"Revive Thy work, O Lord!"* Read again the passages of Scripture at the beginning of the chapter, and see how they all contain the one thought: revival is God's work. He alone can give it; it must come from above. We are frequently in danger of looking at what God *has* done and *is* doing, and to count on that as the pledge that He will at once do more. And all the time He may be blessing us by the measure of our faith or self-sacrifice, and cannot give more until we discover and confess what is hindering Him. Or we may be looking at all the signs of life and good around us. We may be congratulating ourselves on all the organizations and agencies that are being created. All the while, the need of

God's mighty and direct intervention is not properly felt, and entire dependence on Him is not cultivated.

Regeneration—the giving of Divine life—we all acknowledge to be God's act, a miracle of His power. The restoring or reviving of the Divine life, in a soul or a Church, is as much a supernatural work. To have the spiritual discernment that can understand the signs of the heavens, and predict the coming revival, we need to enter deep into God's mind and will. We need God to reveal its conditions, and to prepare those who are to pray for it or are to be used to bring it out. "Surely the Lord God will do nothing, but He revealeth His secret unto His servants the prophets" (Amos 3:7). It is God who is to give the revival. It is God who reveals His secret. It is the spirit of absolute dependence on God, giving Him the honor and the glory, that will prepare for it.

2. *"Revive Thy work, O Lord!"* A second lesson suggested is that the revival God is to give will be given in answer to prayer. It must be asked and received directly from God Himself. Those who know anything about the history of revivals will remember how often this has been proved. Both international and local revivals have been distinctly linked to special prayer. In our own day, there are numerous congregations and missions where special or permanent revivals are—all glory be to God— connected with systematic, believing prayer. The coming revival will be no exception. An extraordinary spirit of prayer—urging believers to much secret and united prayer—pressing them to "labour

fervently" in their supplications, will be one of the surest signs of approaching showers and floods of blessing.

Let all who are burdened by the lack of spirituality, the low state of the life of God in believers, listen to the call that comes to us. If there is to be revival—a mighty, Divine revival—it will need wholeheartedness in prayer and faith. Let not one believer think himself too weak to help, or imagine that he will not be missed. The gift that is in him may be so inspiring that, for his friends or neighborhood, he will be God's chosen intercessor.

Let us think of the need of souls, of all the sins among God's people, of the lack of power in so much of the preaching, and begin to cry, "Wilt Thou not revive us again: that Thy people may rejoice in Thee?" And let us have this truth lodged deep in our hearts: every revival comes, as Pentecost came, as the fruit of united, continued prayer. The coming revival must begin with a great prayer revival. It is in the closet, with the door shut, that the sound of abundant revival will be first heard. An increase in the secret prayer of ministers and members will be the sure herald of blessing.

3. *"Revive Thy work, O Lord!"* A third lesson our texts teach is that the revival is promised to the humble and contrite. We want the revival to break down and save the proud and the self-satisfied. God will give this, but only on the condition that those who see and feel the sin of others take their burden of confession and bear it. All who pray for and claim in

faith God's reviving power for His Church should humble themselves with the confession of its sins. The need of revival always points to previous decline. And the decline was always caused by sin. Humiliation and contrition have always been the conditions for revival. In all intercession, confession of man's sin and God's righteous judgment is always an essential element.

We continually see this throughout the history of Israel. It comes out in the reformations under the pious kings of Judah. We hear it in the prayer of men like Ezra, Nehemiah, and Daniel. In Isaiah, Jeremiah, and Ezekiel, as well as in the minor prophets, it is the keynote of all the warnings and promises. If there is no humiliation and forsaking of sin, there can be no revival or deliverance. "These men have set up their idols in their heart...should I be inquired of at all by them?" (Ezekiel 14:3). "To this man will I look, even to him that is poor and of a contrite spirit, and trembleth at My word" (Isaiah 66:2). Amid the most gracious promises of Divine visitation, there is this note: "Be ashamed and confounded for your own ways, O House of Israel" (Ezekiel 36:32).

We find the same in the New Testament. The Sermon on the Mount promises the Kingdom to the poor and those who mourn. In the Epistles to the Corinthians and Galatians, the religion of man—of worldly wisdom and confidence in the flesh—is exposed and denounced. Without this worldliness being confessed and forsaken, all the promises of grace and the Spirit will be vain. In the Epistles to the seven churches, we find five of which He has something against. In each of these, the keyword of His message is—not to the unconverted, but to the Church—Repent! All the glorious promises which each of these Epistles contain, down to the last one, with its "Open the door, I will come in"; "To him that overcometh will I grant to sit with Me in My throne" (Revelation 3:20-21), are dependent on that one word—Repent!

And if there is to be a revival in our churches, to yield a holy, spiritual membership, won't that trumpet sound need to be heard—Repent? Was it only in Israel, in the ministry of kings and prophets, that there was so much evil in God's people to be cleansed away? Was it only in the Church of the first century that Paul and James and our Lord Himself had to speak such sharp words? Or is there not in the Church of our days an idolatry of money, talent, and culture? Is there not a worldly spirit, making it unfaithful to its one and only Husband and Lord—a confidence in the flesh which grieves and resists God's Holy Spirit? Is there not a confession of the lack of spirituality and spiritual power?

Let all who long for the coming revival, who seek to hasten it by their prayers, pray this above everything—that the Lord may prepare His prophets to go before Him at His bidding. "Cry aloud, spare not, lift up thy voice like a trumpet, and shew My people their transgression" (Isaiah 58:1). Every deep revival among God's people must have

152

its roots in a deep sense and confession of sin. Until those who would lead the Church in the path of revival bear faithful testimony against the sins of the Church, people will be found unprepared.

Men would gladly have a revival as the outgrowth of their agencies and progress. God's way is the opposite. It is out of death, acknowledged as the desert of sin, confessed as utter helplessness, that He revives. He revives the heart of the contrite one.

4. *"Revive Thy work, O Lord!"* There is a final thought suggested by the text from Hosea. It is as we return *to the Lord* that revival will come. For, if we had not wandered from Him, His life would be among us in power. "Come and let us return unto the Lord: for He hath torn, and He will heal us; He hath smitten, and He will bind us up...*He will revive us*...and we shall live in His sight" (Hosea 6:1-2). As we have said, there can be no return to the Lord where there is no sense or confession of wandering. *Let us return to the Lord* must be the keynote of the revival. Let us return, acknowledging and forsaking whatever there has been in the Church that is not entirely according to His mind and spirit. Let us return, yielding up and casting out whatever power of God's two great enemies—confidence in the flesh or the spirit of the world—has been in our faith.

Let us return and acknowledge how undividedly God must have us to fill us with His Spirit, and use us for the Kingdom of His Son. Oh, let us return in the surrender of a dependence and a devotion which has no measure but the absolute claim of Him who is the Lord. Let us return to the Lord with our whole heart, that He may make and keep us wholly His. He will revive us, and we will live in His sight. Let us turn to the God of Pentecost, as Christ led His disciples to turn to Him, and the God of Pentecost will turn to us.

The great work of intercession is needed for this returning to the Lord. It is here that the coming revival must find its strength. Let us begin as individuals to plead with God, confessing whatever we see of sin or hindrance, in ourselves or others. If there were no other sin, surely the lack of prayer is matter enough for repentance, confession, and returning to the Lord. Let us seek to foster the spirit of confession, supplication, and intercession in those around us. Let us help to encourage and train those who think themselves too weak. Let us lift up our voice to proclaim the great truths.

The revival must come from above. It must be received in faith from above and brought down by prayer. The revival comes to the humble and contrite, and it is up to them to bring it to others. If we return to the Lord with our whole heart, He will revive us. On those who see these truths rests the solemn responsibility of giving themselves up to witness for them and to act them out.

And as each of us pleads for the revival throughout the Church, let us especially cry to God for our own neighborhood or sphere of work. Let there be, with every minister and worker, "great searchings of heart" (Judges 5:16), as to whether they are ready to give as much time and strength to prayer as God desires. Let them, even as they are, in public, leaders of their larger or smaller circles, give themselves, in secret, to take their places in the front rank of the great intercession host. They must prevail with God before the great revival, the floods of blessing can come. Of all who speak or think or long for revival, let none hold back in this great work of honest, earnest, definite pleading: "Revive Thy work, O Lord!" "Wilt Thou not revive us again?"

Come and let us return to the Lord. He will revive us! And let us know, let us follow on to know the Lord. "*His going forth* is sure as the morning; and *He shall come unto us* as the rain, as the latter rain that watereth the earth." Amen. So be it.

HELPS TO INTERCESSION

Pray without ceasing. Who can do this? How can one who is surrounded by the cares of daily life do it? How can a mother love her child without ceasing? How can the eyelids protect the eyes without ceasing? How can I breathe, feel, and hear without ceasing? Because all these are the functions of a healthy, natural life. And so, if the spiritual life is healthy—under the full power of the Holy Spirit—praying without ceasing will be natural.

Pray without ceasing. Does it refer to continual acts of prayer in which we are to persevere until we obtain, or to the spirit of prayerfulness that should be with us all day? It includes both. The example of our Lord Jesus shows us this. We have to enter our closet for special seasons of prayer; we are at times to persevere there in importunate prayer. We are also to walk daily in God's presence, with the whole heart set on heavenly things. Without set times of prayer, the spirit of prayer will be dull and feeble. Without the continual prayerfulness, the set times will not avail.

Pray without ceasing. Does that refer to prayer for ourselves or others? To both. It is because many confine it to themselves that they fail so in practicing it. It is only when the branch gives itself to bear fruit—more fruit, much fruit—that it can live a healthy life, and expect a rich inflow of sap. The death of Christ brought Him to the place of everlasting intercession. Your death with Him to sin and self sets you free from the care of self. It elevates you to the dignity of intercessor—one who can get life and blessing from God for others. Know your calling; begin this your work. Give yourself wholly to it, and before you know it you will be finding something of this *"Praying always"* within you.

Pray without ceasing. How can I learn it? The best way to learn how to do a thing—in fact the only way—is *to do it*. Begin by setting apart some time every day, say ten or fifteen minutes, in which you say to God and to yourself that you come to Him now as an intercessor for others. Let it be after your morning or evening prayer, or any other time. If you cannot secure the same time every day, do not be troubled. Only see that you do your work. Christ chose you and appointed you to pray for others.

If at first you do not feel any special urgency or faith or power in your prayers, do not let that hinder you. Quietly tell your Lord Jesus of your feebleness. Believe that the Holy Spirit is in you to teach you to pray, and be assured that if you begin, God will help you. God cannot help you unless you begin and keep on.

Pray without ceasing. How do I know what to pray for? Once you begin, and think of all the needs around you, you will soon find enough. But to help you, follow the subjects and hints for prayer provided in the back of this book. Use it month by month, until you know more fully how to follow the Spirit's leading, and have learned to make your own list of subjects to pray for. A few words may be needed to guide you in the use of these helps.

How to pray. You notice there are two headings for every day—What to Pray and How to Pray. If the subjects were only given, one might fall into the routine of mentioning names and things before God, and the work would become a burden. The hints under the heading, How to Pray, are meant to remind of the spiritual nature of the work—of the need of Divine help—and to encourage faith in the certainty that God, through the Spirit, will give us grace to pray correctly, and will also hear our prayer. One does not at once learn to take his place boldly, and to dare to believe that he will be heard. Therefore, take a few moments each day to listen to God's voice reminding you of how certainly even

157

you will be heard. Hear how He calls on you to pray in that faith in your Father, to claim and take the blessing you plead for. And let these words about how to pray enter your heart and occupy your thoughts at other times, too. The work of intercession is Christ's great work on earth, intrusted to Him because He gave Himself a sacrifice to God for men. The work of intercession is the greatest work a Christian can do. Give yourself a sacrifice to God for men, and the work will become your glory and your joy, too.

What to pray. Scripture calls us to pray for many things: for all saints, for all men, for kings and all rulers, for all who are in adversity, for the sending forth of laborers, for those who labor in the gospel, for all converts, for believers who have fallen into sin, and for one another in our own immediate circles. The Church is now so much larger than when the New Testament was written. The kinds of work and types of workers are so much greater. The needs of the Church and the world are so much better known that we need to take time and thought to see where prayer is needed. We need to discern what our heart is most drawn out to. The Scripture's call to prayer demands a large heart, taking in all saints, all men, and all needs. An attempt has been made in these helps to indicate the chief subjects which need prayer. That ought to interest every Christian.

Many will find it difficult to pray for such large spheres as are sometimes mentioned. Let it be understood that in each case we may make special intercession for our own area of interest which falls under that heading. And it is hardly necessary to say that where one subject appears of more special interest or urgency than another, we are free to take up that subject at any time. If time is really given to intercession, and if the spirit of believing intercession is cultivated, the object is attained. While, on the one hand, the heart must be enlarged at times to take in all, the more pointed and definite our prayer can be the better it is.

Answers to prayer. More than one book has been published in which Christians may keep a register of their petitions, and note when they were answered, so that petitions regarding individual souls or special spheres of work may be recorded, and the answer looked for. When we pray for all saints, or for missions in general, it is difficult to know when or how our prayer is answered, or whether our prayer has had any part in bringing the answer. It is of extreme importance that we prove that God hears us, and to this end take note of what answers we look for, and when they come. On the day of praying for all saints, take the saints in your congregation or in your prayer-meeting, and ask for a revival among them. Take, in connection with missions, some special station or missionary you are interested in, and plead for blessing. And expect and look for its coming, that you may praise God.

Prayer circles. There is no desire in publishing this invitation to intercession to add another prayer group to the many existing fellowships. The first object is to stir the many Christians who—through ignorance or unbelief—take very little part in the work of intercession. The second is to help those who do pray to some fuller understanding of the greatness of the work, and the need of giving their whole strength to it. There is a circle of prayer which asks for prayer on the first day of every month for the fuller manifestation of the power of the Holy Spirit throughout the Church. I have given the words of that invitation as subject for the first day, and taken the same thought as keynote all through. The more one thinks of the need, the promise, and the greatness of the obstacles to be overcome in prayer, the more one feels it must become our life work day by day. It must be that to which every other interest is subordinated.

However, it is suggested that it may be helpful to have small prayer circles to unite in prayer. If a minister were to invite some of his neighboring brethren to join for some special requests along with the printed subjects for supplication, or a number of the more earnest members of his congregation to unite in prayer for revival, some might be trained to take their place in the great work of intercession, who now stand idle because no man has hired them.

Who is sufficient for these things? The more we study and try to practice this grace of intercession, the more we become overwhelmed by its greatness and our feebleness. Let every such impression lead us to listen: My grace is sufficient for thee; and to answer truthfully: Our sufficiency is of God. Take courage; it is in the intercession of Christ you are called to take part. The burden and the agony, the triumph and the victory are all His. Learn from Him. Yield to His Spirit in you, to know how to pray. He gave Himself a sacrifice to God for men, that He might have the right and power of intercession. "He bare the sin of many, and made intercession for the transgressors." Let your faith rest boldly on His finished work. Let your heart wholly identify itself with Him in His death and His life. Like Him, give yourself to God a sacrifice for men: it is your highest nobility; it is your true and full union to Him. It will be to you, as to Him, your power of intercession. Beloved Christian! come and give your whole heart and life to intercession, and you will know its blessedness and its power. God asks nothing less. The world needs nothing less. Christ asks nothing less. Let nothing less be what we offer to God.

FIRST DAY

What to pray—*For the power of the Holy Spirit.*

"I bow my knees unto the Father...that He would grant you...to be strengthened with might by His Spirit"—Ephesians 3:14-16.

"Wait for the promise of the Father"—Acts 1:4.

"The fuller manifestation of the grace and energy of the Blessed Spirit of God, in the removal of all that is contrary to God's revealed will, so that we grieve not the Holy Spirit, but that He may work in mightier power in the Church, for the exaltation of Christ and the blessing of souls."

God has one promise to and through His exalted Son. Our Lord has one gift to His Church. The Church has one need. All prayer unites in the one petition—the power of the Holy Spirit. Make it your one prayer.

How to pray—*As a child asks a father.*

"If a son shall ask bread of any of you that is a father, will he give him a stone?... How much more shall your heavenly Father give the Holy Spirit to them that ask Him?"—Luke 11:11-13.

Ask as simply and trustfully as a child asks bread. You can do this because "God has sent forth the Spirit of His Son into your heart, crying, Abba, Father." This Spirit is in you to give you childlike confidence. In the faith of His praying in you, ask for the power of that Holy Spirit everywhere. Mention places or groups where you specially ask it to be seen.

SECOND DAY

What to pray—*For the Spirit of supplication.*

"The Spirit Itself maketh intercession for us"—Romans 8:26.

"I will pour out...the spirit...of supplications"—Zechariah 12:10.

"The evangelization of the world depends, first of all, on a revival of prayer. Deeper than the need for men—deep down at the bottom of our spiritless life—is the need for the forgotten secret of prevailing, world-wide prayer."

Every child of God has the Holy Spirit in him to pray. God waits to give the Spirit in full measure. Ask for the outpouring of the Spirit of supplication. Ask it for your own prayer circle.

How to pray—*In the Spirit.*

"Praying always with all prayer and supplication in the Spirit"—Ephesians 6:18.

"Praying in the Holy Ghost"—Jude 20.

Our Lord gave the Holy Spirit to His disciples on His resurrection day to enable them to wait for

the full outpouring on the day of Pentecost. It is only
in the power of the Spirit already in us, acknowledged and yielded to, that we can pray for His fuller
manifestation. Say to the Father, the Spirit of His
Son in you is urging you to plead His promise.

THIRD DAY

What to pray—*For all saints.*

*"With all prayer and supplication...and
watching thereunto with all perseverance and supplication for all saints"*—Ephesians 6:18.

Every member of a body is interested in the
welfare of the whole, and exists to help and complete
the others. Believers are one body, and ought to
pray, not so much for the welfare of their own
church or society, but, first of all, for all saints. This
large, unselfish love is the proof that Christ's Spirit
and love is teaching them to pray. Pray first for all
and then for the believers around you.

How to pray—*In the love of the Spirit.*

*"By this shall all men know that ye are My
disciples, if ye have love one to another"*—John
13:35.

*"I pray that they all may be one;...that the
world may believe that Thou hast sent Me"*—John
17:21.

"I beseech you, brethren...for the love of the

Spirit, that ye strive together with me in your prayers to God for me"—Romans 15:30.

"Above all things have fervent love among your selves"—1 Peter 4:8.

If we are to pray we must love. Let us say to God we do love all His saints. Let us say we especially love every child of His we know. Let us pray with fervent love, in the love of the Spirit.

FOURTH DAY

What to pray—*For the Spirit of holiness.*

God is the holy One. His people are holy people. He speaks: I am holy. I am the Lord which make you holy. Christ prayed: Sanctify them. Make them holy through Thy Truth. Paul prayed: "God establish your hearts unblameable in holiness." "God sanctify you wholly!"

Pray for all saints—God's holy ones—throughout the Church. Pray that the Spirit of holiness may rule them—especially pray for new converts. Pray for the saints in your own neighborhood or congregation and for any you are especially interested in. Think of their special need, weakness, or sin, and pray that God may make them holy.

How to pray—*Trusting in God's omnipotence.*

The things that are impossible with men are possible with God. When we think of the great things we ask for, how impossible they seem in light of our insignificance. Prayer is not only wishing or asking, but believing and accepting. Be still before God, and ask Him to let you know Him as the Almighty One. Leave your petitions with Him who works wonders.

FIFTH DAY

What to pray—*That God's people may be kept from the world.*

"Holy Father, keep through Thine own name those whom Thou hast given Me....I pray not that Thou shouldest take them out of the world, but that Thou shouldest keep them from the evil. They are not of the world, even as I am not of the world"— John 17:11,15-16.

In the last night, Christ asked three things for His disciples: that they might be kept as those who are not of the world; that they might be sanctified; that they might be one in love. You cannot do better than to pray as Jesus prayed. Ask that God's people may be kept separate from the world and its spirit; that they, by the Holy Spirit, may live as those who are not of the world.

How to pray—*Having confidence before God.*

"Beloved, if our heart condemn us not, then have we confidence toward God. And whatsoever we ask, we receive of Him, because we keep His command-

ments, and do those things that are pleasing in His sight"—1 John 3:21-22.

Learn these words by heart. Get them into your heart. Join the ranks of those who, with John, draw near to God with an assured heart. Their heart does not condemn them, having confidence toward God. In this spirit, pray for your brother who sins (1 John 5:16). In the quiet confidence of an obedient child, plead for those of your brethren who may be giving way to sin. Pray for all to be kept from evil. And say often, "What we ask, we receive, because we abide and do."

SIXTH DAY

What to pray—*For the Spirit of love in the Church.*

"*I pray . . . that they may be one, even as we are one: I in them, and Thou in Me . . . that the world may know that Thou hast sent Me, and hast loved them, as Thou hast loved Me . . . that the love wherewith Thou hast loved Me may be in them, and I in them*"—John 17:22-26.

"*The fruit of the Spirit is love*"—Galatians 5:22.

Believers are one in Christ, as He is one with the Father. The love of God rests on them, and can dwell in them. Pray that the power of the Holy Spirit may so work this love in believers that the world may see and know God's love in them. Pray much for this.

How to pray—*As one of God's remembrancers.*

"I have set watchmen up on thy walls...which shall never hold their peace day nor night: ye that make mention of the Lord keep not silence, and give Him no rest"—Isaiah 62:6-7.

Study these words until your whole soul be filled with the consciousness, I am appointed intercessor. Enter God's presence in that faith. Study the world's need with that thought—it is my work to intercede. The Holy Spirit will teach you for what and how. Let it be an abiding consciousness. My great life-work, like Christ's, is intercession—to pray for believers and those who do not yet know God.

SEVENTH DAY

What to pray—*For the power of the Holy Spirit in ministers.*

"I beseech you...that ye strive together with me in your prayers to God for me"—Romans 15:30.
"He will yet deliver us; ye also helping together by prayer for us"—2 Corinthians 1:10-11.

What a great host of ministers there are in Christ's Church. What need they have of prayer. What an influence they might be if they were all clothed with the power of the Holy Spirit. Pray definitely for this; long for it. Think of your own minister, and ask it especially for him. Connect every thought of the ministry, in your town, neighborhood, or the world, with the prayer that all may be filled with the Spirit. Plead for them the promise, "Tarry till ye be clothed with power from on high." "Ye shall receive power, when the Holy Ghost is come upon you."

How to pray—*In secret.*

"But thou, when thou prayest, enter into thy closet, and when thou hast shut thy door, pray to thy Father which is in secret"—Matthew 6:6.

"He departed again into a mountain to pray, Himself alone"—Matthew 14:23; John 6:15.

Take time and realize when you are alone with God: here I am now, face to face with God, to intercede for His servants. Do not think you have no influence, or that your prayer will not be missed. Your prayer and faith will make a difference. Cry in secret to God for His ministers.

EIGHTH DAY

What to pray—*For the Spirit in all Christian workers.*

"Ye also helping together by prayer for us, that for the gift bestowed upon us by means of many persons thanks may be given by many on our behalf"—2 Corinthians 1:11.

What multitudes of workers in our churches, missions, railways, government offices, armed forces, schools, businesses, hospitals, and community organizations. God be praised for this! How much they would accomplish if each were living in the fullness of the Holy Spirit. Pray for them; it makes you a partner in their work, and you will praise God each time you hear of blessing anywhere.

How to pray—*With definite petitions.*

"What wilt thou that I should do unto thee?"— Luke 18:41.

The Lord knew what the man wanted, and yet He asked him. The utterance of our wish emphasizes our petitions to God, and so awakens faith and expectation. Be very definite in your petitions so as to know what answer to look for. Just think of the great host of workers, and ask and expect God to definitely bless them in answer to the prayers of His people. Then ask still more definitely for workers around you. Intercession is not the breathing out of pious wishes. Its aim is, in believing, persevering prayer, to receive and bring about blessing.

NINTH DAY

What to pray—*For God's Spirit on our mission work.*

"As they ministered to the Lord, and fasted, the

*Holy Ghost said, Separate Me Barnabas and Saul
...and when they had fasted and prayed...they
sent them away. So they, being sent forth by the
Holy Ghost, departed*"—Acts 13:2-4.

"The evangelization of the world depends, first
of all, on a revival of prayer. Deeper than the need
for men—deep down at the bottom of our spiritless
life—is the need for the forgotten secret of prevailing, world-wide prayer."

Pray that our mission work may all be done in
this spirit—waiting on God, hearing the voice of the
Spirit, sending forth men with fasting and prayer.
Pray that in our churches our mission interest and
mission work may be in the power of the Holy Spirit
and of prayer. A Spirit-filled, praying Church will
send out Spirit-filled missionaries, mighty in prayer.

How to pray—*Take time.*

"*I give myself unto prayer*"—Psalm 109:4.

"*We will give ourselves continually to
prayer*"—Acts 6:4.

"*Be not rash with thy mouth, and let not thine
heart be hasty to utter anything before God*"—
Ecclesiastes 5:2.

"*And He continued all night in prayer to
God*"—Luke 6:12.

Time is one of the prime estimates of value. The
time we give is a proof of the interest we feel.

We need time with God—to realize His presence; to wait for Him to make Himself known; to consider and feel the needs we plead for; to take our place in Christ; to pray until we can believe that we have received. Take time in prayer, and pray for blessing on the mission work of the Church.

TENTH DAY

What to pray—*For God's Spirit
on our missionaries.*

"Ye shall receive power, after that the Holy Ghost is come upon you: and ye shall be witnesses unto Me . . . unto the uttermost parts of the earth"—Acts 1:8.

What the world needs today is not only more missionaries, but the outpouring of God's Spirit on everyone whom He has sent out to work for Him in the foreign field.

God always gives His servants power equal to the work He asks of them. Think of the greatness and difficulty of this work—casting Satan out of his strongholds—and pray that everyone who takes part in it may receive and do all His work in the power of the Holy Spirit. Think of the difficulties of your missionaries, and pray for them.

How to pray—*Trusting God's faithfulness.*

"He is faithful that promised . . . She judged

Him faithful who had promised"—Hebrews 10:23;
11:11.

Just think of God's promises to His Son concerning His Kingdom; to the Church concerning the heathen; to His servants concerning their work; to yourself concerning your prayer; and pray in the assurance that He is faithful. He only waits for prayer and faith to fulfill them. "Faithful is He that calleth you" (to pray), "who also will do it" (what He has promised.)

Take up individual missionaries, make yourself one with them, and pray until you know that you are heard. O begin to live for Christ's Kingdom as the one thing worth living for!

ELEVENTH DAY

What to pray—*For more laborers.*

"Pray ye therefore the Lord of the harvest, that He will send forth laborers into His harvest"—Matthew 9:38.

What a remarkable call by the Lord Jesus for help from His disciples in getting the need supplied. What an honor put on prayer. What a proof that God wants prayer and will hear it.

Pray for laborers, for all students in theological seminaries, training homes, Bible institutes, that

173

they may not go unless He fits them and sends them forth. Pray that our churches may train their students to seek for the sending forth of the Holy Spirit. Pray that all believers may hold themselves ready to be sent forth, or to pray for those who can go.

How to pray—*In faith, nothing doubting.*

"Jesus answering saith unto them, Have faith in God....Whosoever shall say unto this mountain, Be thou removed, and be thou cast into the sea; and shall not doubt in his heart, but shall believe that those things which he saith shall come to pass; he shall have whatsoever he saith"—Mark 11:22-23.

Have faith in God! Ask Him to make Himself known to you as the faithful, mighty God who works all in all. And, you will be encouraged to believe that He can give suitable and sufficient laborers, however impossible this appears. But, remember, He does so in answer to prayer and faith.

Apply this to every opening where a good worker is needed. The work is God's. He can give the right workman. But He must be asked and waited on.

TWELFTH DAY

What to pray—*For the Spirit to convict the world of sin.*

"I will send the Comforter unto you. And when He is come, will reprove the world of sin"—John 16:7-8.

God's one desire—the one object of Christ's being manifested—is to take away sin. The first work of the Spirit in the world is the conviction of sin. Without that, no deep or abiding revival, no powerful conversion can come about. Pray for it, that the gospel may be preached in such power of the Spirit, that men may see that they have rejected and crucified Christ, and cry out, "What will we do?"

Pray most earnestly for a mighty power of the conviction of sin wherever the gospel is preached.

How to pray—*Stir up yourself to take hold of God's strength.*

"Let him take hold of My strength, that he may make peace with Me"—Isaiah 27:5.

"There is none that calleth upon Thy name, that stirreth up himself to take hold of Thee"—Isaiah 64:7.

"Stir up the gift of God, which is in thee"—2 Timothy 1:6.

First, take hold of God's strength. God is a Spirit. I cannot take hold of Him, and hold Him fast, except by the Spirit. Take hold of God's strength, and hold on until it has done for you what He has promised. Pray for the power of the Spirit to convict of sin.

Second, stir up yourself the power that is in you by the Holy Spirit to take hold. Give your whole heart and will to it, and say, "I will not let Thee go except Thou bless me."

THIRTEENTH DAY

What to pray—*For the Spirit of burning.*

"And it shall come to pass, that he that is left in Zion...shall be called holy...when the Lord shall have washed away the filth of the daughters of Zion...by the spirit of judgment, and by the spirit of burning"—Isaiah 4:3-4.

A washing by fire! a cleansing by judgment! he who has passed through this will be called holy. The power of blessing for the world, the power of work and intercession that will avail, depends on the spiritual state of the Church. And, that can only rise higher as sin is discovered and put away. Judgment must begin at the house of God. There must be conviction of sin for sanctification. Beseech God to give His Spirit as a spirit of judgment and a spirit of burning—to discover and burn out sin in His people.

How to pray—*In the Name of Christ.*

"Whatsoever ye shall ask in My name, that will I do...If ye shall ask Me any thing in My name, I will do it"—John 14:13-14.

Ask in the Name of your Redeemer God, who sits on the throne. Ask what He has promised, what He gave His blood for, so that sin may be put away from among His people. Ask—the prayer is after His own heart—for the spirit of deep conviction of sin to come among His people. Ask for the spirit of burning. Ask in the faith of His Name—the faith of what He wills, of what He can do—and look for the answer. Pray that the Church may be blessed, to be made a blessing in the world.

FOURTEENTH DAY

What to pray—*For the Church of the future.*

"That the children might not be as their fathers...a generation that set not their heart aright, and whose spirit was not steadfast with God"—Psalm 78:8.

"I will pour My Spirit upon thy seed, and My blessing upon thine offspring"—Isaiah 44:3.

Pray for the rising generation who are to come after us. Think of the young men, women, and children of this age, and pray for all the agencies at work among them. Pray that in associations, societies, and unions, in homes and schools, Christ may be honored, and the Holy Spirit get possession of them. Pray for the young of your own neighborhood.

How to pray—*With the whole heart.*

"The Lord grant thee according to thine own heart"—Psalm 20:4.

"Thou hast given him his heart's desire"—Psalm 21:2.

"I cried with my whole heart; hear me, O Lord"—Psalm 119:145.

God lives and listens to every petition with His whole heart. Each time we pray, the whole Infinite God is there to hear. He asks that in each prayer the whole man be there, too. He asks that we cry with our whole heart. Christ gave Himself to God for men. And so, He takes up every need into His intercession. If once we seek God with our whole heart, the whole heart will be in every prayer with which we come to God. Pray with your whole heart for the young.

FIFTEENTH DAY

What to pray—*For schools and colleges.*

"As for Me, this is My covenant with them, saith the Lord; My Spirit that is upon thee, and My words which I have put in thy mouth, shall not depart out of thy mouth, nor out of the mouth of thy seed, nor out of the mouth of thy seed's seed, saith the Lord, from henceforth and for ever"—Isaiah 59:21.

The future of the Church and the world depends, to an extent we little conceive, on the education of the day. The Church may be seeking to evangelize the heathen, and be giving up her own children to secular and materialistic influences. Pray for schools and colleges, and that the Church may realize and fulfill its momentous duty of caring for its children. Pray for godly teachers.

How to pray—*Not limiting God.*

"They...limited the Holy One of Israel"—Psalm 78:41.

"He did not many mighty works there because of their unbelief"—Matthew 13:58.

"Is anything too hard for the Lord?"—Genesis 18:14.

"Ah, Lord God! Thou hast made the heaven and the earth by Thy great power...there is nothing too hard for Thee. Behold, I am the Lord...is there anything too hard for Me?"—Jeremiah 32:17,27.

Beware, in your prayer, above everything, of limiting God, not only by unbelief, but by fancying that you know what He can do. Expect unexpected things, above all that we might ask or think. Each time you intercede, be quiet first and worship God in His glory. Think of what He can do, of how He delights to hear Christ, of your place in Christ, and expect great things.

SIXTEENTH DAY

What to pray—*For the power of the
Holy Spirit in our Sunday schools.*

*"Thus saith the Lord, Even the captives of the
mighty shall be taken away, and the prey of the
terrible shall be delivered: for I will contend with
him that contendeth with thee, and I will save thy
children"*—Isaiah 49:25.

Every part of the work of God's Church is His
work. He must do it. Prayer is the confession that He
will, if we surrender ourselves into His hands, work
in us and *through* us. Pray for the hundreds of
thousands of Sunday school teachers, that those
who know God may be filled with His Spirit. Pray
for your own Sunday school. Pray for the salvation
of the children.

How to pray—*Boldly.*

*"We have a great High Priest . . . Jesus the Son
of God . . . Let us therefore come boldly unto the
throne of grace"*—Hebrews 4:14,16.

These hints to help us in our work of
intercession—what are they doing for us? Making us
conscious of our weakness in prayer. Thank God for
this. It is the very first lesson we need on the way to
pray the effectual prayer that avails much. Let us
persevere, taking each subject boldly to the throne of
grace. As we pray, we will learn to pray, to believe,

and to expect with increasing boldness. Hold fast your assurance: it is at God's command you come as an intercessor. Christ will give you grace to pray correctly.

SEVENTEENTH DAY

What to pray—*For kings and rulers.*

"I exhort therefore, that, first of all, supplications, prayers, intercessions, and giving of thanks, be made for all men; for kings, and for all that are in authority; that we may lead a quiet and peaceable life in all godliness and honesty"—1 Timothy 2:1-2.

What a faith in the power of prayer! A few weak and despised Christians are to influence the mighty Roman emperors, and help in securing peace and quietness. Let us believe that prayer is a power that is taken up by God in His rule of the world. Let us pray for our country and its rulers. Let us pray for all the rulers of the world—for the rulers in cities or districts in which we are interested. When God's people unite in this, they may count on their prayer effecting the unseen world more than they know. Let faith hold this fast.

How to pray—*The prayer before God as incense.*

"And another angel came and stood at the altar,

having a golden censer; and there was given unto him much incense, that he should offer it with the prayers of all the saints upon the golden altar which was before the throne. And the smoke of the incense which came with the prayers of the saints, ascended up before God out of the angel's hand. And the angel took the censer, and filled it with fire of the altar, and cast it into the earth: and there were voices, and thunderings, and lightnings, and an earthquake"— Revelation 8:3-5.

The same censer brings the prayer of the saints before God and casts fire on the earth. The prayers that go up to heaven have their share in the history of this earth. Be sure that your prayers enter God's presence.

EIGHTEENTH DAY

What to pray—*For peace.*

"I exhort therefore, that, first of all, supplications be made for . . . kings and all that are in authority; that we may lead a quiet and peaceable life in all godliness and honesty. For this is good and acceptable in the sight of God our Saviour"—1 Timothy 2:1-3.

"He maketh wars to cease unto the end of the earth"—Psalm 46:9.

What a terrible sight—the military armaments

in which the nations find their pride! What a terrible thought—the evil passions that may at any moment bring on war! And what a prospect—the suffering and desolation that must come! God can, in answer to the prayer of His people, give peace. Let us pray for it, and for the rule of righteousness on which alone it can be established.

How to pray—*With the understanding.*

"What is it then? I will pray with the spirit, and I will pray with the understanding"—1 Corinthians 14:15.

We need to pray with the spirit, as the vehicle of the intercession of God's Spirit, if we are to take hold of God in faith and power. We need to pray with the understanding, if we are really to enter deeply into the needs we bring before Him. Take time to understand intelligently, in each subject, the nature, the extent, the urgency of the request, the ground, way, and certainty of God's promise as revealed in His Word. Let the mind affect the heart. Pray with the understanding and with the Spirit.

NINETEENTH DAY

What to pray—For the *Holy Spirit on Christendom.*

"Having a form of godliness, but denying the power thereof"—2 Timothy 3:5.

"Thou hast a name that thou livest, and art dead"—Revelation 3:1.

There are five hundred million nominal Christians. The state of the majority is unspeakably awful. Formality, worldliness, ungodliness, rejection of Christ's service, ignorance, and indifference—to what an extent does all this prevail. We pray for the heathen—do let us pray for those bearing Christ's name, many are in worse than heathen darkness.

Do you not feel as if you ought to begin to give up your life, and to cry day and night to God for souls? In answer to prayer, God gives the power of the Holy Spirit.

How to pray—*In deep stillness of soul.*

"My soul waiteth upon God: from Him cometh my salvation"—Psalm 62:1.

Prayer has its power in God alone. The nearer a man comes to God Himself, the deeper he enters into God's will. The more he takes hold of God, the more power in prayer.

God must reveal Himself. If it pleases Him to make Himself known, He can make the heart conscious of His presence. Our posture must be that of holy reverence, of quiet waiting and adoration.

As your month of intercession passes on, and you feel the greatness of your work, be still before God. Thus you will get power to pray.

TWENTIETH DAY

What to pray—*For God's Spirit on the heathen.*

"*Behold, these shall come from far . . . and these from the land of Sinim*"—Isaiah 49:12.

"*Princes shall come out of Egypt; Ethiopia shall soon stretch out her hands unto God*"—Psalm 68:31.

"*I the Lord will hasten it in His time*"—Isaiah 60:22.

Pray for the heathen, who are yet without the Word. Think of China, with her three hundred million—a million a month dying without Christ. Think of Africa, with its two hundred million. Think of thirty million a year going down into the darkness. If Christ gave His life for them, will you do the same? You can give yourself up to intercede for them. Just begin, if you have never begun, with this simple, monthly school of intercession. The ten minutes you give will make you feel this is not enough. God's Spirit will draw you on. Persevere, however weak you are. Ask God to give you some country or group of people to pray for. Can anything be nobler than to do as Christ did? Give your life for the heathen.

How to pray—*With confident expectation of an answer.*

"*Call unto Me, and I will answer thee, and shew thee great and mighty things, which thou knowest not"*—Jeremiah 33:3.

"Thus saith the Lord God; I will yet for this be inquired of . . . to do it"—Ezekiel 36:37.

Both texts refer to promises definitely made, but their fulfillment would depend on prayer—God would be inquired of to do it.

Pray for God's fulfillment of His promises to His Son and His Church, and expect the answer. Plead for the heathen. Plead God's promises.

TWENTY-FIRST DAY

What to pray—*For God's Spirit on the Jews.*

"I will pour out upon the house of David, and upon the inhabitants of Jerusalem, the Spirit of grace and of supplications: and they shall look upon Me whom they have pierced"—Zechariah 12:10.

"Brethren, my heart's desire and prayer to God for Israel is, that they may be saved"—Romans 10:1.

Pray for the Jews. Their return to the God of their fathers stands connected, in a way we cannot tell, with wonderful blessing to the Church, and with the coming of our Lord Jesus. Do not think that God has foreordained all this, and that we cannot hasten it. In a Divine and mysterious way, God has connected His fulfillment of His promise with our prayer. His Spirit's intercession in us is God's fore-runner of blessing. Pray for Israel and the work done among them. Even so, come, Lord Jesus! Amen.

How to pray—*With the intercession of the Holy Spirit.*

"We know not what we should pray for as we ought; but the Spirit Itself maketh intercession for us with groanings which cannot be uttered"—Romans 8:26.

In your ignorance and weakness, believe in the secret indwelling and intercession of the Holy Spirit within you. Yield yourself to His life and leading habitually. He will help your infirmities in prayer. Plead the promises of God even where you do not see how they are to be fulfilled. God knows the mind of the Spirit, because He makes intercession for the saints according to the will of God. Pray with the simplicity of a little child. Pray with the holy awe and reverence of one in whom God's Spirit dwells and prays.

TWENTY-SECOND DAY

What to pray—*For all who are in suffering.*

"Remember them that are in bonds, as bound with them; and them which suffer adversity, as being yourselves in the body"—Hebrews 13:3.

What a world of suffering we live in! How Jesus sacrificed all and identified Himself with it! Let us in our measure do so, too. The persecuted Russians, Poles, and Germans, the famine stricken millions of India, the poverty and wretchedness of our great cities—and so much more. What suffering among those who know God and do not know Him. And then, in ten thousand homes and hearts, what sorrow. In our own neighborhood, how many need help or comfort. Let us have a heart for, let us think of, the suffering. It will stir us to pray, to work, to hope, to love more. And in an unknown way and time, God will hear our prayer.

How to pray—*Praying always, and not fainting.*

"He spake a parable unto them to this end, that men ought always to pray, and not to faint"—Luke 18:1.

Do you not begin to feel that prayer is really the help for this sinful world? What a need there is of unceasing prayer. The very greatness of the task makes us despair! What can our ten minutes of intercession avail? It is right we feel this. This is the way in which God is calling and preparing us to give our life to prayer. Give yourself wholly to God for men, and, amid all your work, your heart will be drawn out to men in love, drawn up to God in dependence and expectation. To a heart thus led by the Holy Spirit, it is possible to pray always and not to faint.

188

TWENTY-THIRD DAY

What to pray—*For the Holy Spirit in your own work.*

"I also labor, striving according to His working, which worketh in me mightily"—Colossians 1:29.

You have your own special work—make it a work of intercession. Paul labored, striving according to the working of God in him. Remember, God is not only the Creator, but the great Workman, who works all in all. You can only do your work in His strength, by Him working in you through the Spirit. Intercede much for those among whom you work, until God gives you life for them.

Let us all intercede, too, for each other—for every worker throughout God's Church, however solitary or unknown.

How to pray—*In God's very presence.*

"Draw nigh to God, and He will draw nigh to you"—James 4:8.

The nearness of God gives rest and power in prayer. The nearness of God is given to him who makes it his first object. "Draw nigh to God"; seek the nearness to Him, and He will give it; "He will draw nigh to you." Then it becomes easy to pray in faith.

Remember that when God first takes you into the school of intercession it is almost more for your own sake than that of others. You have to be trained to love, wait, pray, and believe. Only persevere. Learn to set yourself in His presence, to wait quietly for the assurance that He draws near. Enter into His holy presence, remain there, and spread your work before Him. Intercede for the souls you are working among. Receive a blessing from God—His Spirit into your own heart—for them.

TWENTY-FOURTH DAY

What to pray—*For the Spirit on your own congregation.*

"Beginning at Jerusalem"—Luke 24:47.

Each one of us is connected with some congregation or circle of believers. They are to us the part of Christ's body with which we come into most direct contact. They have a special claim on our intercession. Let it be a settled matter between God and you that you are to labor in prayer on its behalf. Pray for the minister and all leaders or workers in it. Pray for the believers according to their needs. Pray for conversions. Pray for the power of the Spirit to manifest itself. Band yourself with others to join in definite petitions. Let intercession be a definite work, carried on as systematically as preaching or Sunday school. And pray, expecting an answer.

How to pray—*Continually.*

"*Watchmen...which shall never hold their peace day nor night*"—Isaiah 62:6.

"*His own elect, which cry day and night unto Him*"—Luke 18:7.

"*Night and day praying exceedingly that we might...perfect that which is lacking in your faith*"—1 Thessalonians 3:10.

"*A widow indeed...trusteth in God, and continueth in supplications...night and day*"—1 Timothy 5:5.

When the glory of God, the love of Christ, and the need of souls are revealed to us, the fire of this unceasing intercession will begin to burn in us for those who are near and those who are far off.

TWENTY-FIFTH DAY

What to pray—*For more conversions.*

"*He is able also to save them to the uttermost ...seeing He ever liveth to make intercession*"—Hebrews 7:25.

"*We will give ourselves continually to prayer, and to the ministry of the word.... And the word of God increased; and the number of the disciples multiplied*"—Acts 6:4,7.

Christ's power to save, and save completely, depends on His unceasing intercession. The apostles' withdrawing of themselves from other work to give themselves continually to prayer was followed by the number of the disciples multiplying exceedingly. As we, in our day, give ourselves to intercession, we will have more and mightier conversions. Let us plead for this. Christ is exalted to give repentance. The Church exists with the Divine purpose and promise of having conversions. Let us not be ashamed to confess our sin and feebleness, and cry to God for more conversions in Christian and heathen lands, and of those whom you know and love. Plead for the salvation of sinners.

How to pray—*In deep humility.*

"Truth, Lord: yet the dogs eat of the crumbs.... O woman, great is thy faith: be it unto thee even as thou wilt"—Matthew 15:27-28.

You feel unworthy and unable to pray correctly. To accept this heartily, and to be content still to come and be blest in your unworthiness is true humility. It proves its integrity by not seeking for anything, but simply trusting His grace. And so it is the very strength of a great faith, and gets a full answer. "Yet the dogs"—let that be your plea as you persevere for someone possibly possessed by the devil. Do not let your littleness hinder you for a moment.

TWENTY-SIXTH DAY

What to pray—*For the Holy Spirit on young converts.*

"Peter and John...prayed for them, that they might receive the Holy Ghost: for as yet He was fallen upon none of them: only they were baptized in the name of the Lord Jesus"—Acts 8:15-16.

"Now He which stablisheth us with you in Christ, and hath anointed us, is God; who hath also...given the earnest of the Spirit in our hearts"—2 Corinthians 1:21-22.

How many new converts remain feeble. How many fall into sin. How many backslide entirely. If we pray for the Church, its growth in holiness and devotion to God's service, pray especially for the young converts. How many stand alone, surrounded by temptation. How many have no teaching on the Spirit in them, and the power of God to establish them. How many in persecuted lands, surrounded by Satan's power. If you pray for the power of the Spirit in the Church, pray especially that every young convert may know that he may claim and receive the fullness of the Spirit.

How to pray—*Without ceasing.*

"As for me, God forbid that I should sin against the Lord in ceasing to pray for you"—1 Samuel 12:23.

It is a sin to cease praying for others. When we begin to see how absolutely indispensable intercession is, just as much a duty as loving God or believing in Christ, and how we are called and bound to it as believers, we will feel that to cease intercession is grievous sin. Let us ask for grace to take up our place as priests with joy, and give our life to bring down the blessing of heaven.

TWENTY-SEVENTH DAY

What to pray—*That God's people may realize their calling.*

"I will bless thee...and thou shalt be a blessing ...In thee shall all families of the earth be blessed"—Genesis 12:2-3.

"God be merciful unto us, and bless us; and cause His face to shine upon us. That Thy way may be known upon earth, Thy saving health among all nations"—Psalm 67:1-2.

Abraham was only blessed that he might be a blessing to all the earth. Israel prays for blessing, that God may be known among all nations. Every believer, just as much as Abraham, is only blessed so that he may carry God's blessing to the world.

Cry to God that His people may know this— that every believer is only to live for the interests of God and His Kingdom. If this truth were preached, believed, and practiced, what a revolution it would bring in our mission work. What a host of willing intercessors we would have. Plead with God to work it by the Holy Spirit.

How to pray—*As one who has accepted for himself what he asks for others.*

"Peter said...such as I have, give I thee.... The Holy Ghost fell on them, as on us at the beginning .... God gave them the like gift as He did unto us"—Acts 3:6; 11:15,17.

As you pray for this great blessing on God's people, the Holy Spirit taking entire possession of them for God's service, yield yourself to God, and claim the gift anew in faith. Let each thought of weakness or shortcoming only make you more urgent in prayer for others. As the blessing comes to them, you, too, will be helped. With every prayer for conversions or mission work, pray that God's people may know how wholly they belong to Him.

TWENTY-EIGHTH DAY

What to pray—*That all God's people may know the Holy Spirit.*

"The Spirit of truth; whom the world...neither knoweth: but ye know Him; for He dwelleth with you, and shall be in you"—John 14:17.

"Know ye not that your body is the temple of the Holy Ghost?"—1 Corinthians 6:19.

The Holy Spirit is the power of God for the salvation of men. He only works as He dwells in the Church. He is given to enable believers to live wholly as God would have them live, in the full experience and witness of Him who saves completely. Pray God that every one of His people may know the Holy Spirit! Pray that He, in all His fullness, is given to them! Pray that they do not expect to live as their Father would have without having Him in His fullness, without being filled with Him! Pray that all God's people everywhere may learn to say: I believe in the Holy Spirit.

How to pray—*Laboring fervently in prayer.*

"Epaphras,who is one of you . . . saluteth you, always laboring fervently for you in prayers, that ye may stand perfect and complete in all the will of God"—Colossians 4:12.

To a healthy man labor is a delight; in what interests him he labors fervently. The believer who is in full health, whose heart is filled with God's Spirit, labors fervently in prayer. For what? That his brethren may stand perfect and complete in all the will of God. That they may know what God wills for them, how He calls them to live, be led, and walk by the Holy Spirit. Labor fervently in prayer that all God's children may know this, as possible, as Divinely sure.

TWENTY-NINTH DAY

What to pray—*For the Spirit of intercession.*

"I have chosen you, and ordained you, that ye should go and bring forth fruit . . . that whatsoever ye shall ask of the Father in My name, He may give it you"—John 15:16.

"Hitherto ye have asked nothing in My name . . . At that day ye shall ask in My name"—John 16:24-26.

Has not our school of intercession taught us how little we have prayed in the name of Jesus? He promised His disciples: "In that day, when the Holy Spirit comes upon you, ye shall ask in My name." Are there not tens of thousands with us mourning the lack of the power of intercession? Let our intercession today be for them and all God's children, that Christ may teach us through the Holy Spirit in us what it is to live in His fullness, and to yield ourselves to His intercession work within us. The Church and the world need nothing so much as a mighty Spirit of Intercession to bring down the power of God on earth. Pray for the descent from heaven of the Spirit of Intercession for a great prayer revival.

How to pray—*Abiding in Christ.*

"If ye abide in Me, and My words abide in you, ye shall ask what ye will, and it shall be done unto you"—John 15:7.

Our acceptance by God, our access to Him, is all in Christ. As we consciously abide in Him we have the liberty—not a liberty to our old nature or our self-will, but the Divine liberty from all self-will—to ask what we will, in the power of the new nature, and it will be done. Let us keep this place, believe even now that our intercession is heard, and that the Spirit of supplication will be given all around us.

THIRTIETH DAY

What to pray—*For the Holy Spirit
with the Word of God.*

"Our gospel came not unto you in word only, but also in power, and in the Holy Ghost, and in much assurance"—1 Thessalonians 1:5.

"Those who preached unto you the gospel with the Holy Ghost sent down from heaven"—1 Peter 1:12.

So many Bibles are being circulated. So many sermons on the Bible are being preached. So many Bibles are being read in homes and schools. How little blessing when it comes "in word" only; what Divine blessing and power when it comes "in the Holy Ghost," when it is preached "with the Holy Ghost sent forth from heaven." Pray for Bible circulation, and preaching, teaching, and reading, that it may all be in the Holy Spirit, with much prayer.

Pray for the power of the Spirit with the Word in your own neighborhood, wherever it is being read or heard. Let every mention of "the Word of God" awaken intercession.

How to pray—*Watching and praying.*

"Continue in prayer, and watch in the same with thanksgiving; withal praying also for us, that God would open unto us a door for the word"—Colossians 4:2-3.

Do you not see how all depends on God and prayer? As long as He lives, loves, hears, and works, as long as there are souls with hearts closed to the Word, as long as there is work to be done in carrying the Word—Pray without ceasing. Continue steadfastly in prayer, watching therein with thanksgiving. These words are for every Christian.

THIRTY-FIRST DAY

What to pray—*For the Spirit
of Christ in His people.*

"I am the Vine, ye are the branches"—John 15:5.

"That ye should do as I have done to you"—John 13:15.

As branches we are to be so like the Vine, so

entirely identified with it, that all may see that we have the same nature, life, and spirit. When we pray for the Spirit, let us not only think of a Spirit of power, but the very disposition and temper of Christ Jesus. Ask and expect nothing less. For your self, and all God's children, cry for it.

How to pray—*Striving in prayer.*

"That ye strive together with me in your prayers to God for me"—Romans 15:30.

"I would that ye knew what great conflict I have for you"—Colossians 2:1.

All the powers of evil seek to hinder us in prayer. Prayer is a conflict with opposing forces. It needs the whole heart and all our strength. May God give us grace to strive in prayer until we prevail.

THE MINISTRY OF INTERCESSION

God's ministers are many,
  For this His gracious will,
Remembrancers that day and night
  This holy office fill.
While some are hushed in slumber,
  Some to fresh service wake,
And thus the saintly number
  No change or chance can break.
And thus the sacred courses
  Are evermore fulfilled,
The tide of grace by time or place
  Is never stayed or stilled.

Oh, if our ears were opened
  To hear as angels do
The Intercession-chorus
  Arising full and true,
We should hear it soft up-welling
  In morning's pearly light;
Through evening's shadows swelling
  In grandly gathering might;
The sultry silence filling
  Of noontide's thunderous glow,
And the solemn starlight thrilling
  With ever-deepening flow.

We should hear it through the rushing
  Of the city's restless roar,
And trace its gentle gushing

O'er ocean's crystal floor:
We should hear it far up-floating
   Beneath the Orient moon,
And catch the golden noting
   From the busy Western noon;
And pine-robed heights would echo
   As the mystic chant up-floats,
And the sunny plain resound again
   With the myriad-mingling notes.

Who are the blessed ministers
   Of this world-gathering band?
All who have learnt one language,
   Through each far-parted land;
All who have learnt the story
   Of Jesus' love and grace,
And are longing for His glory
   To shine in every face.
All who have known the Father
   In Jesus Christ our Lord.
And know the might and love the light
   Of the Spirit in the Word.

Yet there are some who see not
   Their calling high and grand,
Who seldom pass the portals,
   And never boldly stand
Before the golden altar
   On the crimson-stained floor,
Who wait afar and falter,
   And dare not hope for more.

Will ye not join the blessed ranks
  In their beautiful array?
Let intercession blend with thanks
  As ye minister today!

There are hands too often weary
  With the business of the day,
With God-entrusted duties,
  Who are toiling while they pray.
They bear the golden vials,
  And the golden harps of praise
Through all the daily trials,
  Through all the dusty ways,
These hands, so tired, so faithful,
  With odors sweet are filled,
And in the ministry of prayer
  Are wonderfully skilled.

There are ministers unlettered,
  Not of Earth's great and wise,
Yet mighty and unfettered
  Their eagle-prayers arise.
Free of the heavenly storehouse!
  For they hold the master-key
That opens all the fullness
  Of God's great treasury.
They bring the needs of others,
  And all things are their own,
For their one grand claim is Jesus' Name
  Before their Father's throne.

So the incense-cloud ascendeth
    As through calm, crystal air,
A pillar reaching unto heaven
    Of wreathed faith and prayer.
For evermore the Angel
    Of intercession stands
In His Divine Priesthood
    With fragrance-filled hands,
To wave the golden censer
    Before His Father's throne,
With Spirit-fire intenser,
    And incense all His own.

And evermore the Father
    Sends radiantly down
All-marvelous responses,
    His ministers to crown;
The incense-cloud returning
    As golden blessing-showers,
We in each drop discerning
    Some feeble prayer of ours,
Transmuted into wealth unpriced,
    By Him who giveth thus
The glory all to Jesus Christ,
    The gladness all to us!

—F. R. Havergal